What Other Leaders
Pointers in Proverbs

I've always found Jim's *Pointers* to be insightful and worth the time. Management can be reduced to techniques, decision trees and spreadsheets. Consistent and principled leadership, however, is in short supply and Jim shows how the wisdom from a few thousand years ago applies today just as it did then.

TIM BROWN
Former VP of a major automotive supplier,
West Point Class of 1968

I have been reading Jim's *Pointers* for several years. I look forward to each issue because they are both inspiring and thought-provoking.

DAVID A COLE
CPA

There are plenty of 'how to' books for life and business. Some are based on knowledge and experience. While these are good things, they still are not as valuable as wisdom. Wisdom is far deeper and enduring. Pointers in Proverbs uses eternal wisdom to develop men and women into **wise** leaders; something that our world today desperately needs.

RANDY COOPER
Electrical Contractor

Pointers in Proverbs brings life and light from the Eternal Word into our daily lives. Jim Furr helps ordinary folks see that Eternal Life can start in our lives by reading, thinking and doing our daily work in accordance with God's Word.

MYLES J CROWE
CPA, CFP, Registered Principal, West Point Class of 1968

I so enjoy Jim's essays. Glad to know that through this book others will have an opportunity to see God's wisdom in action.

BEV DAVIS
Senior Managing Director, national healthcare provider

In *Pointers in Proverbs,* Jim mines timeless gems of biblical wisdom from the book of Proverbs and skillfully polishes them for current day understanding and application. Each short essay encourages the reader to strengthen aspects of Christ-like character within themselves, which, in turn positively influences others around them as well.

CRAIG GEORGE
Former CEO, Company Founder, Director and Author

If you desire to live life with excellence then you MUST read these essays, each of which expands on the insights of one or more verses from the Bible book of Proverbs. This book will help men and women become more values-based in their leadership.

CHUCK GIASSON
Senior Consultant, Suss Consulting, Inc.,
West Point Class of 1968

As a cadet at West Point, I attended mandatory chapel. Years later I realized those Sunday morning sermons helped me to learn to live a life with excellence. For a number of years now, Jim's *Pointers in Proverbs* have continue that learning and I realize how I am blessed with reading each of his essays.

RICK GOODELL
Ass't Chief, Operations Division, Portland District at
US Army Corps of Engineers, West Point Class of 1968

For believers–and seekers, non-believers, ponderers and spiritual wanderers–Jim's messages lucidly convey insights for all of us: compassion, justice, charity and forgiveness for our fellow life travellers.

HENRY GREGOR
MD, West Point Class of 1968

Jim's *Pointers in Proverbs* are thoughtful, challenging, actionable nuggets designed to point us to Jesus so we can live our life with His wisdom, peace and grace.

MIKE HENRY SR,
VP, Information Technology, SageNet LLC

I never cease to be inspired by Jim's thoughtful reflections on the scriptures. His ability to integrate his personal experiences and current events into his essays lend a timely and personal touch to these biblical passages. He is an inspiration for all who believe in the Lord Jesus Christ and all he has done for us.

CHICK JAMES
MD, West Point Class of 1968

I've always loved Jim's *Pointers in Proverbs*.

MIKE KIMBREL
President, Kimbrel Oil

Jim's *Pointers in Proverbs* are well-written and I love the use of stories combined with the truths of Proverbs to provide such practical applications for life. Jim's writing clearly shows he is a teacher at heart with a desire and ability to articulately communicate the truth of the Bible.

CHRIS KOERNER
Client Services

For the Past two months, I have been receiving Jim Furr's *Pointers in Proverbs.* They have inspired me and caused me to rethink and retain certain proverbs. Frequently the message hits home to me during the week that I read it. It will be great to have in book form!!!

PETER LUITWIELER
VP, Supply and Logistics, and CIO (Ret.), CITGO Petroleum

The *Pointers* are a regular way for me to stay grounded in the working world. I see practical ways that God is trying to help me do my job better and make a consistent witness in my office both with staff and patients.

TOM MIHELICH
MD

For many years, I have been receiving and pondering Jim's *Pointers in Proverbs*. They are fundamentally based and compelling in their content.

JAMES C MIZELL
MD

Jim Furr's *Pointers in Proverbs* have provided me with excellent words of wisdom in dealing with the multiple problems facing all of us in these turbulent times. I would highly recommend his collection of essays.

ART SANDS
MD, West Point Class of 1968

Over years of reading *Pointers in Proverbs* I have found them to be a clear and concise exhortation to thoughtfully consider and then apply in our daily lives the valuable truths of God's timeless wisdom set forth in the Proverbs.

LARRY SHEPPARD
Petroleum Engineer

Pointers in Proverbs has in innumerable instances provided me helpful guidance in reflecting on difficult issues. Day-to-day living can often be confounding and complicated.

It has been supportive and spiritually renewing to glean wisdom and understanding from these essays.

PATRICK STRONG
West Point Class of 1968

For many years now, *Pointers in Proverbs* have provided a steady stream of insights on understanding God and living life well. I've looked forward to these essays each month, and now I look forward to having them in one collection!

CLAY THOMPSON
Sr. Director, Walmart

Jim has a gift for seeing how the bible both reflects and addresses everyday life. When he applies God's communication to the issues we all face, God is not a pronouncer of mistakes but a friend showing us the way to our deepest dreams. And who doesn't want that?

DAVID WILLIAMS
Cru City Staff

For Dave —
Thanks for your friendship & for
your partnership in helping fulfill
the Great Commission. May you
always choose wisdom!. —
Pr 8:10 & 11
Best wishes,
Jim Furr
4/20/16

POINTERS
IN PROVERBS

Wisdom to Live and Lead with Excellence

DR. JIM FURR

Dedication

To my West Point Class of 1968
friends and colleagues.
When gathered with these men,
I'm in the company of heroes.

And to Ginny's and my grandchildren
with a prayer that they will follow
the principles outlined in Proverbs
and throughout the Bible
and become godly leaders
in their generation.

Contents

Contents

Foreword

The Old Testament Book of Proverbs, written by King Solomon of Israel and some other wise men of his time, 950 to 700 BC, is a profound guide for gaining wisdom in life.

A few years ago, Dr. Jim Furr, a friend and spiritual counselor, gave me a fascinating version of the Bible entitled, *The Leadership Bible* (General Editor Dr. Sid Buzzell). It draws out and highlights leadership lessons from the scriptures. It points out that anyone aspiring to be a leader can benefit from the insights in the *Book of Proverbs*.

In his *Pointers in Proverbs* Jim Furr presents us with life examples of the wisdom and guidance found in selected verses from the *Book of Proverbs*. Jim's essays show how the guidance and the wisdom found in the Proverbs apply to contemporary issues. His essays expand the insights of the Proverbs and thus are of added value, not only to leaders and aspiring leaders, but also to anyone desiring to lead a good and fruitful Christian life.

As a West Point graduate, a Vietnam veteran, a Doctor of Ministry, a teaching pastor for 17 years, and since 2001, a FocalPoint (Cru) Team Leader, Jim has deeply rooted experience in leadership development. His *Pointers* complement Jim's FocalPoint ministry, in which he is supported by his bride of 46 years, Ginny. FocalPoint brings together professional and business men and women in a quest to create Christ-centered leaders in their endeavors. Jim and Ginny have six adult children and nine grandchildren.

Read and enjoy Jim's *Pointers in Proverbs*. I did and I keep looking forward to each new essay.

Nick Krawciw
West Point Class of 1959
Once a soldier

Acknowledgments

These essays would not have been written without the constant encouragement of my wife, Ginny. Ginny has also been the editor for the *Pointers* over the past 15+ years. In addition, she has helped me stay true to the "seeker" tone and tenor of the series.

There are a number of men and women that have championed the publication of *Pointers in Proverbs*. Their enthusiasm played a key role in persuading me to undertake this project. Rather than attempt to list everyone by name – I'd be sure to overlook some – my thanks to all for their kind and constructive words.

Special thanks to Randy Cooper, among the most vocal for publication, for his editing efforts with the manuscript and to West Point classmate Chuck Giasson for his invaluable help with the organization of the essays.

Introduction

One day early in 2000, West Point classmate and friend Sam Brooks phoned with an invitation to a mini-reunion he was hosting. Sam was anxious to introduce his new bride to a group of his West Point friends and their wives. So that September, Ginny and I flew from our home in Oklahoma to Washington, DC for what would be three fun-filled days with Sam and Diane and 20+ other couples at the Brooks' Arlington Virginia home.

Despite not having seen most of these classmates for over 30 years and the fact that we came disguised with bulges, bifocals and baldness, I felt an immediate bond with these men that I had come to know so well through the 47-month crucible that is West Point.

After our return to Tulsa, Ginny and I reflected on conversations with different ones during that weekend. While it was apparent that some of these special friends were Christ-followers, it occurred to us that others possibly were not.

I was anxious to help my friends discover the Bible's relevance for their lives, as I had some five years following graduation from West Point, and to share with them the good news of God's offer of forgiveness through faith in his Son, Jesus. This desire led to a biweekly "blog" in which I determined to do my best to avoid clichés and the assumption that my readers had a Bible background. My objective would be to offer a simple explanation of how God's wisdom in Proverbs intersects with life in the 21st century.

Thus in October 2000 I launched *Pointers in Proverbs*, a series of essays that I continue today to write and email to many of those classmates who attended that mini-reunion in 2000 and to a number of other business and professional men and women. Each essay ties into and expands on one or more proverbs that challenge us to pursue wisdom in some area of our personal and professional lives.

The 60 essays that follow are a collection of more recent articles appearing in the *Pointers* series. They are organized by the four categories into which they naturally fall. Category 1 consists of 17 essays describing qualities of a good leader, such as revealing others' value, listening deeply, and transcending self.

The 20 essays in Category 2 outline the actions and attitudes that lead to a life of excellence. Here you will find articles on winning others' respect, maintaining slack, and answering the higher call.

Category 3's 15 essays focus on assertions Proverbs makes about "truth" as presented in the scriptures. Included in this section are articles discussing the Bible's superiority to conventional wisdom, its trustworthiness as a life guide, and its record of holding up under intense scrutiny.

Finally, eight essays make up Category 4. Included here are articles explaining how hope, peace and security are found, for example, through understanding God's character, accepting God's purpose for suffering, and facing and forgiving hurts.

The first of two appendices, Appendix A is My Faith Story. Appendix B, Reflections, explains how one may know God personally.

All author royalties from *Pointers in Proverbs* go to fund FocalPoint, a movement dedicated to helping marketplace and professional men and women develop their leadership and life skills through application of biblical principles.

Jim Furr
Team Leader
FocalPoint Tulsa

The Essays
Category 1

*Nothing happens apart from leadership, and
everything rises and falls on leadership.*
– John Maxwell

Essays 1-17:

A good leader...

...is dedicated to a noble cause

Essay 1: What Are You Committed To?

History teaches that those who change the world are not the best educated, the wealthiest, or even the most talented. World changers are the folks with the deepest dedication to a cause–good or evil. Jesus Christ was born into poverty and had no formal education, but today over a billion people follow his teachings. In 1939, 100,000 young men and women crammed into a stadium in Munich, Germany. They were all wearing brown shirts, and with their bodies they together formed a sign that read, "Hitler, we are yours." They nearly took over the world.

Asserting the power of commitment, leadership guru John Maxwell writes, "Commitment always precedes achievement. I am told that in the Kentucky Derby the winning horse effectively runs out of oxygen after the first half mile, and he goes the rest of the way on heart. NBA legend Michael Jordan explains that 'heart is what separates the good from the great.'"

In sharp contrast to the high achievement of the committed is the sheer helplessness of the sluggard, as illustrated in the Bible book of Proverbs. It says for example in 26:15, "The sluggard buries his hand in the dish; he is too lazy to bring it back to his mouth." This metaphor depicts a life without commitment. For the sluggard the rare effort of beginning becomes too much; the impulse dies. His meal goes cold on him.

Unfortunately, there are some in our culture today who like the proverbial sluggard won't commit to anything. "I want to keep my options open;" "I haven't decided yet;" "I'm still thinking about it," are phrases heard too often these days. Why do so many young people–and not-so-young people, too–opt to just live together instead of getting married? Simply put, they don't want to make a long-term commitment.

So what are you and I committed to? I'm confident that, like me, you want to finish well, make a difference right up to the end. The trouble is that the older we get the tougher it is to muster the effort it takes to keep on going for the gold. You know what I'm talking about? What we need is a cause that grabs us by the jugular and energizes us.

Frankly, at one time money did that for me, sort of. It doesn't anymore. Nor does success, prestige, possessions, or impressing people. You may well feel the same way. So where do we find a cause noble enough to capture our imagination and sustain, even revive, our commitment? I'd like to suggest God's cause.

The Bible claims that God is in the life-changing business: that he specializes in offering hope to the hopeless and power to resurrect dead marriages and conquer habits, hang-ups and fears; and that he exchanges peace for anxiety, heals hurts and transforms eternal destinies. "That's my cause," God says, "and nothing would please me more than for you to partner in it with me."

Wow! Now that's something worth rolling out of bed for. There is, however, a price to be paid. The Bible explains that partnership with God & Son Inc. requires giving top billing to God and his purpose. Our desires, relationships, career, golf game – probably all good things. But God's looking to enlist folks who will put him ahead of everything else. "That's a tall commitment," you say. True, but it's been my experience that nothing satisfies like being part of what God's doing in people's lives.

...reveals others' value

Essay 2: Building Others' Esteem

Without advantages like a solid education, adequate financial assets and good health, life can be a real challenge, but without hope, life quickly becomes unsustainable. In the ancient book of Proverbs it says, "A healthy spirit conquers adversity, but what can you do when the spirit is crushed?" (18:14).

I think most of us would agree that to cultivate a healthy spirit requires encouragement and lots of it. In today's fast-paced, highly competitive, oft impersonal world, we all experience losses, disappointments and loneliness. This stuff can cause us to begin doubting our value, which leads to discouragement. That's why maintaining regular contact with people who build us up is critical for our emotional health.

I've found it helpful to keep an encouragement file. When somebody writes me a note, even if it's only mildly encouraging, like, "Good try, Jim. Better luck next time," I file it. On days when I need a lift, I'll sometimes pull out this file that I've kept over the years, and as I read *both* cards over and over, it's fulfilling to me to know that at least sometime in my life my wife and my mother thought I had value. :-)

So we need to be encouraged, but as leaders we understand that the effectiveness of our leadership may well depend on our ability to refresh the spirit of a demoralized follower. How then can we help others recognize their value?

One way, of course, is to verbally affirm them. Like the bride who brings her new husband dinner and says, "Honey, my two specialties are meatballs and peach pie." And her appreciative husband says, "And which is this, darling." You know, he wanted to affirm her.

Better, though, to affirm somebody for who they *are* than just for what they *do*. Psychiatrists who study the power of affirmation have assigned a point value to positive and negative strokes. They tell us that to give somebody a positive stroke for doing something good is worth one point, but to give them a positive stroke for who they are (e.g., "Thanks for being honest," or, "That was a courageous thing you did"), that's a 10. On the other hand, to criticize somebody for something they've done wrong counts as a minus 10, but to criticize them for who they are ("Why are you so dumb?") is a minus 100.

Another way to increase others' self-esteem is illustrated by Saint Paul in the Bible. It seems that Paul had a colleague named Timothy, who by nature was easily intimidated. But it says that Paul took his friend under his wing and invited Timothy to join him as he traveled around the world starting new churches. One day while they were in the city of Ephesus, Paul said, "Tim, I'm going to leave you here, and until I get back, you're in charge of the Ephesian church." Paul trusted his protégée with responsibility, and it changed Timothy's life. In fact, young Tim progressed into one of early Christianity's most capable leaders.

What made the difference was that Paul believed in Timothy more than Timothy believed in himself. Paul kept assigning his colleague responsibilities and expecting the best from him. Finally, with his mentor's encouragement and some hard work Timothy developed confidence in his leadership skills.

Former British Prime Minister Benjamin Disraeli once said, "The greatest good you can do for another is not just to share your riches, but to reveal to him his own." Clearly the best leaders are those who look at people-building as an essential aspect of their job description.

...unleashes those worthy

Essay 3: Empowerment & Integrity

Empowerment is the goal of many leadership initiatives today. We are encouraged to find potential leaders and unleash their talents through equipping them to lead, giving them authority, and then turning them loose to achieve. "The best executive," Theodore Roosevelt noted, "is the one who has sense enough to pick good men to do what he wants done, and self-restraint enough to keep from meddling with them while they do it."

Henry Ford's Model T changed the face of twentieth-century American life. By 1914, Ford was producing nearly 50% of all cars in the U.S. But by the early 1930s Ford's share of the market had shrunk to 28%, and the company was losing a million dollars a day (big bucks, then!). The reason an American success story went south? Henry Ford. The antithesis of an empowering leader, Ford micromanaged his subordinates and undermined the authority of any executive he viewed as a threat to his control.

Abraham Lincoln, on the other hand, observed the principle of empowerment as consistently as Henry Ford violated it. During the Civil War, Lincoln continued to give his commanding generals power and freedom to act, even when this strategy had failed with their predecessors. Eventually, of course, the wisdom of this approach proved itself, Lincoln finding in Grant a recipient worthy of his confidence. As leadership guru John Maxwell points out, "Only empowered people can reach their full potential."

So how do we select worthy candidates to empower? Proverbs 17:2 speaks clearly to this issue: "A wise servant will rule over a disgraceful son, and will share the inheritance as one of the brothers." This verse stresses that the most important qualification for empowerment is not connections, credentials, charm or confidence ("servant" / "son"), but character ("wise" / "disgraceful"). Author Warren Bennis says it like this: "Successful leadership is not about being tough or soft, sensitive or assertive, but about a set of attributes. First and foremost is character."

Makes sense doesn't it. The obvious danger in empowering somebody is that they will abuse their power. So when it's time to promote, men and women of character get the nod, right? Well, unfortunately, not always. Leaders sometimes do what the ancient prophet Samuel did.

The Bible records the story. God commissions Samuel to travel to the home of an Israelite named Jesse and inform one of Jesse's eight sons that he is to become Israel's king elect. When Samuel arrives, in the dark as to the identity of the one he is to anoint, he is naturally drawn to the most photogenic kid, the proven warrior, the one with experience. But God says, "Wrong choice, Sam. It's the boy out shepherding the sheep that I've chosen to be king, the one they call David." David didn't have the connections, credentials, charm or confidence, but he had character. He was a man after God's own heart, and that's what God was looking for in a leader.

We can tend to be like Samuel can't we, ready to empower folks based on outward stuff, instead of what's on the inside. So Proverbs 17:2 reminds us that when it comes to empowering folks to assume a leadership position, what matters most is three things: integrity, integrity, integrity.

A final word on empowerment. It turns out that the principle of empowerment illuminates a key distinction between the Christian faith and "religion." Christianity is sometimes mistaken for a religious system that features a cosmic killjoy God who randomly tells people to do this and not to do that. The reality is far different. According to the ancient scriptures, the Christian faith is about empowerment, not rules. God offers those who trust in Jesus power to improve their character–their integrity–thus enabling them to take their leadership to a new level.

...is guided by virtue

Essay 4: Values-Based Leadership

*According to the polls, in American today there is widespread dissatisfaction with our country's leadership. Real Clear Politics, for example, reported last week that only 44.7% of Americans approve of President Obama's job performance. As weak as that is, Congress' approval rating is far worse, a dismal 17.7%. Moreover, these same polls reveal that our confidence in the other institutions and groups we have traditionally depended on for leadership is likewise trending downward. It would seem a good idea, therefore, to consider what we ought to look for in those who would be our leaders.

Because history everywhere confirms that deficient leadership is not a new phenomenon, it's no surprise to find that Israel's King Solomon, asserted to be the wisest of men, commented some 3,000 years ago on how to avoid poor leadership. My plan in this article is to quote from Solomon's words, then in support of his viewpoint to cite an example of a good leader who is well known to all of us.

In Proverbs, Solomon writes, "Righteousness exalts a nation, but sin is a disgrace to any people" (14:34). He says that virtue exalts a nation. In other words, values-based leadership inspires and ennobles a group of people. On the other hand, Solomon warns that anything less than values-based leadership, although it might appear in the short run to be working, ultimately has a corrupting effect on people.

"Wanted – A Leader!" screamed the headline in the "New York Times" a week after Fort Sumter fell in 1861 to Confederate troops marking the onset of the Civil War. The article went on to declare that only a great leader may prevent a great crisis from resulting in "disaster and defeat." In the "Times" opinion Abraham Lincoln was spectacularly unqualified to fill that role.

Clearly there was reason to question the qualifications of the little-known Illinois attorney. At a moment in American's history when wisdom was essential, Lincoln himself admitted that his education had been defective. He had little legislative experience, and the largest staff he had ever managed was his junior partner and a few clerks in his law office. Yet, somehow he rose to the occasion, eventually emerging as one of the greatest leaders of this or any other nation.

How was this possible? I would suggest to you that while it's true that Lincoln grew into his daunting job, his development into a superb leader was not due to some miracle makeover. The truth is that undergirding and energizing the development of his competence as president were remarkable values-based leadership qualities. Here are three.

Courageous. In a speech in New York that launched his run for the presidency, Lincoln addressed restricting slavery. "Let us have faith," he counseled, "that right makes might." At the very outset of his campaign he wanted his position on this highly controversial issue to be clear. Lincoln didn't need a political poll to tell him what was right. In his view it was right to restrict slavery, and he believed that "right" would give them the might to do so.

Humble. George McClellan, the Union Army commander in 1861, was arrogant, snobbish and at times even insubordinate to the president. On one such occasion Lincoln's Secretary of State, William Seward, was enraged when McClellan clearly snubbed his commander-in-chief. But Lincoln told Seward, "I'll hold McClellan's horse if he'll only bring us success."

Compassionate. Under pressure to exact extreme retribution from a defeated Confederacy, Lincoln, although crushing the South was within his power, made it clear that he did not intend to seek revenge. "On the whole," he said, "my impression is that mercy bears richer fruits than any other attribute."

Why are we today facing what many describe as a leadership crisis in America? Could it be that in our preoccupation with finding leaders who are competent we have ignored the more important qualification of virtue?

*With assistance from a John Maxwell talk entitled "Values Based Leadership"

...praises others

Essay 5: Appreciating Others' Contributions

Years ago, a young man walked into a diner and asked to use a pay phone (you remember those?). The waitress behind the counter pointed him in the right direction and then eavesdropped as he made his call.

Once connected to his party, the young man said in an enthusiastic voice, "Hello, Mr. Anderson. My name is Patrick DeBerg, and I was calling to ask whether you'd be interested in hiring a bright, hardworking sales manager to oversee your marketing staff.... Oh, I see. You already have a bright, hardworking sales manager. Well, thanks anyway."

The young man walked back to the counter with a smug grin on his face. Perplexed, the waitress asked, "What are you smiling about? You just got turned down."

"Well, actually," the young man replied, "I didn't. You see, I'm that 'bright, hardworking sales manager.' I just wanted to make sure that my boss thought so too."

Mike Zigarelli cites this scenario in his book, "Management by Proverbs," to make the point that people are eager to know that others appreciate their contribution. According to Zigarelli, research indicates that employees are motivated by recognition more than almost anything else. They want fair pay and job security, but they also crave hearing that they're doing a good job, something bosses too often fail to tell them.

The Bible, which I would contend provides the most thorough treatment of leadership to be found anywhere, supplies helpful insights on showing appreciation for others' efforts. For instance, in describing the ideal wife Proverbs 31 notes that in addition to being skilled in crafts of home and hearth, she rises before dawn to organize her day, runs a profitable business, speaks with insight, is quick to assist the needy, etc. How is such a woman to be rewarded? Verses 30 and 31 explain: "Charm is deceptive and beauty is fleeting; but a woman who fears the Lord is to be praised. Give her the reward she has earned, and let her works bring her praise at the city gate."

Notice it doesn't say that this amazing worker should get a merit raise, a new Lexus chariot or a weekend at the Jerusalem spa. Any of these things might well be an appropriate way to express recognition of her value, but first and foremost she deserves praise.

Furthermore, the reason she is to be praised is because she has "earned" it. Hmm.... Could it be that acknowledgment of someone's accomplishments is as much management's responsibility as a paycheck? ... that appreciation is something folks are entitled to? No doubt. Little wonder long-term failure to praise can result in bitterness.

Finally, we're told in the Proverb that praise should be offered "at the city gate." That is, the ideal wife was to be rewarded in a high traffic area. Recognition of others' contributions, in other words, is best done publicly so that everybody is made aware of what has been achieved.

In "Love Works," author Joel Manby, CEO of Herschend Family Entertainment, captures another aspect of the importance of appreciating others' contributions in his chapter on kindness. He writes that this sort of thing "is contagious and increases the energy, effectiveness, and productivity in any organization."

I suspect that in the past we've all blown lots of opportunities to show our appreciation to someone by complimenting him or her in the presence of others for a contribution they made to the organization (or to our family!). That said, there's no time like the present to determine, going forward, to do a better job of looking to take advantage of such opportunities.

35

...uses fitting words

Essay 6: Words Aptly Spoken

We can all think of words that we shouldn't have spoken, words that we would give anything to recall. Sometimes we even say, in shame and regret over some comment we sent out to offend and sting, "I take back what I said," but we can never really take it back can we. The damage is done. "We can pluck out the thorn," Peter Marshall writes, "but the pain of it lingers."

We also know that the effectiveness of our leadership in the marketplace, our home, wherever, depends largely on our ability to say the right thing at the right time. Our words will either evoke trust or distrust in those we lead. They will either instill confidence or fear. They will either nurture or destroy. To a great extent our words determine how eagerly our followers will follow us.

The Bible book of James warns us about the potential for death and destruction that's packed into our words, a fact most of us are already aware of both intuitively and through personal experience. James writes, "The tongue is a fire, a world of evil. . . no man can tame the tongue; it is a restless evil, full of deadly poison." And we say, Yes, James, we know. The sobering thing about words, Peter Marshall again, "is that before you speak them, you are their master. After you speak them, they are your master."

With the above as context, I'd like to explore with you briefly a verse in Proverbs that sounds a much happier note on all this. Proverbs 25:11 reads, "A word aptly spoken is like apples of gold in settings of silver." Whatever this metaphor means – and people have different thoughts about that – it's obviously telling us that "aptly spoken" words are a really good thing, in sharp contrast to the "tongue is a fire" idea. So what are words "aptly spoken"?

Surely an example from history of such words is found in Winston Churchill's speech on 20 August 1940. Referring to the heroic work of the R.A.F during the Battle of Britain, when the German air force hurled its might against England, the Prime Minister said, "Never in the field of human conflict was so much owed by so many to so few." I'd suggest to you that this probably couldn't have been said any better. Churchill was indeed a master of the aptly spoken word.

So was Lincoln. We're all familiar with the Gettysburg address. Less known but just as powerful are Lincoln's words in a letter to a Mrs. Bixby of Boston. She had lost five sons in the war. After confessing that any effort on his part to comfort one who had experienced such overwhelming loss was certain to be "fruitless," Lincoln wrote, "I pray that our Heavenly Father may assuage the anguish of your bereavement, and leave you only the cherished memory of the loved and lost, and the solemn pride that must be yours to have laid so costly a sacrifice upon the altar of freedom." What words could possibly improve on that?

Although most of us are unlikely to ever possess the capacity of a Churchill or a Lincoln for saying just the right thing at just the right time, Proverbs 25:11 holds out hope that we may experience significant development in this area. How? While we cannot tame the destructive nature of our tongue, the Bible tells us that God can. Another proverb calls a tongue that is directed by God a rare jewel. To put it differently, whatever natural ability we possess to share words of praise, courage, hope, peace, and, when appropriate, of warning and rebuke, to those willing to turn to him for help, God has pledged to empower them to take that ability to the next level and beyond.

...is self-aware

Essay 7: Know Thyself

"The purposes of a man's heart are deep waters, but a man of understanding draws them out"–Proverbs 20:5

In the midst of an exciting time for her company, a young CEO unexpectedly quit. Growing up, during her alcoholic parents' frequent fights, she would hide under the bed till the police came. Later, when her board was divided, unable to handle it, she resigned, unaware that her decision was tethered to her past.

Great leaders have a high degree of self-awareness. They know their strengths and have insight into how to deploy them toward the challenges of their role and how to mitigate their weaknesses.

Proverbs 20:5 declares that the purposes of our heart lie deep within and must be drawn out if we are to be aware of them. In his book "Impact," organizational psychologist and management consultant Tim Irwin discusses this drawing out process using the metaphor of three windows of self-awareness: the open self, blind areas and hidden areas. Irwin suggests ways to enlarge our open window while diminishing the blind and hidden areas.

The one "window" through which who we are on the inside is clearly seen by both ourselves and others is what Irwin calls our "open self." Enlarging the open-self window increases our self-awareness, and the greater our self-awareness, the greater our personal authenticity and more effective our leadership.

Take for example Bill Foote, cited by Michael Zigarelli in "Management by Proverbs." Bill stood before 150 managers to deliver his first speech after becoming CEO Of USG Corporation, a building products manufacturer in Chicago.

He opened by telling the traumatic and intensely personal story of his wife's struggle with cancer, which had ended with her death one month before Bill was named CEO.

Now shouldering the new roles of widower, single parent of three young girls and chief executive, Bill Foote elected to stand before his management team and willingly disclose who he was. Later, "The Wall Street Journal" reported that: "As managers talked afterwards...the clear message was 'if we have to go through a few walls for this guy, we're going to do it.'"

The second of Irwin's windows of self-awareness is what he calls the "blind" window. We're all familiar with the concept of blind spots (according to the experts, all leaders have "3.4" of them). Like a car that we collide with because it was in the blind spot of our side-view mirror, personal blind spots can wreck us. The blind window represents areas of our behavior, seen by others but not by us, that limit the effectiveness of our leadership.

To enlarge our open window by diminishing our blind window requires that we have people around us that we've given permission to speak to us with uncensored openness. All of our current and former spouses, for instance. A man was driving home from a gala at which he had received a prestigious award. He mused with his wife, "I wonder how many truly great men there are in the world today?" Her response: "One less than you think."

Irwin's third window of self-awareness he calls the "hidden" window. This window includes areas of our lives that, without intentional effort, neither we nor others see. Hidden defects may not show up for years, then all of sudden they manifest. Consider for example disgraced former NY Congressman Anthony Weiner. Confronted with evidence of lewd behavior, Weiner said, "If you're looking for some kind of deep explanation for it, I simply don't have one except that I'm sorry."

Whatever Weiner's hidden imperfection was – maybe he actually believed the "Cosmopolitan" magazine article acclaiming him one of the "101 Gorgeous Real Life Bachelors" – he needed to discover it, make it part of his open self, then guard against it. You and I need to do that, too. How do we discover these hidden personality flaws? Irwin suggests regular and thoughtful times of introspection. I've found it helpful to include God in these times by reading and prayerfully reflecting on his scriptures.

...leverages power for others

Essay 8: "Beyond You" Leadership

"It is not good to eat too much honey, nor is it honorable to seek one's own honor"–Proverbs 25:27.

Years ago, I had the enlightening experience of conducting two case studies, each focusing on the CEO of a company. For the sake of this article we'll call these companies A and B. I spent several days at each site interviewing the chief executive, his direct reports, and 30 rank and file members of the organization. I observed the CEO's leadership style and how he related with his staff and others within the organization.

My research revealed that while these two companies were in the same type of business and of comparable size, and that talented staffs surrounded both executives, Company A was scrambling just to maintain the status quo, while Company B was growing rapidly. In Company A, the plateaued organization, several of the staff voiced frustration with their CEO, and in general there was an attitude of "our best days are probably behind us." In contrast, within Company B optimism and job satisfaction reigned.

I concluded that the difference in the performance of these two organizations was essentially a function of leadership. Company A was led by an executive with the tendency Israel's King Solomon warned against in Proverbs 25:27. The other CEO was a "beyond you leader." Allow me to explain.

It's no secret that many leaders enjoy making most of the decisions that affect the organization, having others defer to them in meetings, occupying a corner office, "running the show." In other words, they "seek their own honor," which the proverb compares to eating too much honey. Sweet as honey is, and healthy as it is in moderation, too much of it makes us sick. While honor accompanies a job well done, a good thing, for a leader to focus on seeking honor for himself is too much of a good thing and makes for a sick leader.

Company A's CEO tried to do virtually everything. He was controlling and seemed a bit paranoid. Among his direct reports morale was low and frustration high. Because the CEO was determined to "seek his own honor" his staff felt hampered in their efforts to make a significant contribution to the company.

Company B's executive, on the other hand, was a "beyond you leader" (BYL), a description that I became acquainted with only recently. At Leadercast Live 2014, leadership communicator Andy Stanley defined BYLs as leaders who fearlessly and selflessly empower leaders around them as well as those coming along behind them.

Stanley outlined three ways that BYLs leverage their power for the benefit of those around them. One, they refuse to make decisions others can make. When possible the BYL says to his people, "You decide" (I've tried saying this lately, and while it still feels somewhat awkward, I'm beginning to like it). Two, according to Stanley, the BYL makes a habit of working for the team. He asks, "How can I use my power to help you get done what I hired you to do?" Then, third, the BYL empties his cup, meaning that he pours into others what he knows, making certain his people know what he knows about what they are working on.

Although my case study write up did not refer to Company B's executive as a BYL, had I at the time been familiar with this terminology it would have. Based both on what his people told me and what I witnessed, that's the kind of fearless, selfless, empowering leader he was. It's also the kind of leader that you and I should strive to be. For, as Andy Stanley concluded, if our leadership is *not* all about us, it will live beyond us. But if it is all about us, the only way it will live beyond us is in serving as somebody's illustration of a bad example.

...avoids hazards of pride

Essay 9: The Most Dangerous Mistakes Leaders Make

What are the most dangerous mistakes that leaders make? Patrick Lencioni, author of ten business books with more than three million copies sold, spoke to this topic recently at a leadership summit that I attended. What follows is a recounting of Lencioni's "most dangerous mistakes I see leaders make" plus comments of my own.

Becoming a leader for the wrong reason, according to Lencioni, is one mistake leaders commonly make. More than a few go into leadership because of what they believe being the leader will do for them. In Lencioni's view people who become leaders for wrong reasons – power, money, fame– eventually run out of idealism, get bored and leave behind a trail of tears. Lencioni: "If it's not servant leadership, it's just economics."

Author and Taylor University president Eugene Habecker writes, "The true leader serves people, serves their best interests...because true leaders are motivated by loving concern rather than a desire for personal glory." According to Proverbs 20:28, "Love and truth form a good leader."

In the Bible, Jesus, surely in terms of lasting impact history's most successful leader, did not assume a leadership role because he was on a power trip or wanted more stuff. On the contrary, he dissociated himself from those things then became a leader as a means of serving. Lencioni: "The most successful leaders sacrifice themselves for the benefit of others."

Leadership mistake number two: Failing to embrace vulnerability. Lencioni recounted a meeting he had sat in on with a high-powered CEO and his direct reports, who had recently submitted written evaluations of their boss' leadership skills.

"It says here," began the CEO, reading from their evaluations, "that I'm not a good listener. Well, I feel I'm doing better with that. What do you guys think?" Unanimous agreement with the CEO. It went on like that for a while. Finally, at Lencioni's prompting, one of the VPs admitted that he believed the CEO did have areas in need of improvement. His colleagues all disagreed, leaving that VP twisting in the wind.

"The CEO destroyed the trust of his people," said Lencioni, adding that not long afterward that corporation's board fired the CEO due to the company's poor performance. Lencioni: "People have the right to expect us to be competent, but I don't think you can be too vulnerable." "A mocker resents correction, he will not consult the wise" – Proverbs 15:12.

Leadership mistake number three: Making leadership too important. Lencioni: "Our identity can be so wrapped up in our leadership role at work that we ignore our primary constituents." Dare we ask our wife, "Do you think my job and my employees are more important to me than you are?" Lencioni again: "At life's end what counts most is not that employees come around our bed and say what a great leader we are."

In Ecclesiastes King Solomon records his observations of a certain senior executive: "A solitary person, completely alone–no children, no family, no friends–yet working obsessively late into the night." "Why," this guy asks himself, "am I working like a dog, never having any fun? And who cares?'" Solomon's summary of the situation: "How pointless and depressing."

Why do leaders fall into these traps, each of which can lead to disaster? Lencioni: "It's all pride. The antidote is humility." "Pride goes before destruction, a haughty spirit before a fall" – Proverbs 16:18.

So how does a leader, especially who sees himself as successful due to his own efforts, develop humility? He remembers who changed his diapers as a baby, who taught him how to read and write, who nursed him through his illnesses, who gave him his first job, who believed in him enough to promote him. Then he leans into God's power for help in breaking old patterns of behavior.

...strives for unity

Essay 10: Crucial Conversations

"A gentle response turns away wrath, but a harsh word stirs up anger" – Proverbs 15:1

Recently, as I listened to Joseph Grenny present at a seminar from his book, "Crucial Conversations," I thought, "Wow, what a relevant topic!" All of us find ourselves from time to time wanting to bring up important, potentially controversial information at meetings, speak with a direct report about his or her subpar performance, or bring up a sensitive matter with our spouse. On occasion, possibly with fear and trembling, we've initiated these conversations, and sure enough it went poorly. Perhaps more often, we did nothing because we refused to choose between telling the truth and keeping a friend, unaware that, as Grenny notes, "a third choice is available through dialogue." My point is who of us can't use a tip or two on how to be more effective negotiators and conflict resolvers?

My intention in this article is to outline the basic argument of Grenny's book and to compare his conclusions with the perspective of ancient wisdom on this critical topic.

According to Grenny, if we are to master the art of fruitful dialogue in conversations where the stakes are high, emotions are heightened, and opinions differ, we must know what we want the outcome to be for ourselves and for the others involved. Makes sense, but what is the most desirable outcome of a crucial conversation? It's that we win and the other guy lose, right? No, I think most of us would probably agree that the best we could hope for from a critical conversation is not that it all go our way, but that the conversation result in more unity and greater productivity.

Conflict produces energy, energy that can be channeled in a positive direction (or not). A conflict between a husband and wife can serve to facilitate open, honest discussion, which can lead to greater understanding between the two and a better relationship. Similarly, a conflict between two engineers over the design of a product can lead to a better design than either one was capable of producing alone.

So, the goal of crucial conversations is to channel the energy of conflict in the right direction. How do we do that? Ancient wisdom says, "With all humility and gentleness, with patience, make every effort to keep the unity of the Spirit in the bond of peace" (from the Bible book of Ephesians). The assertion here is that approaching conflict with an attitude of humility, gentleness, and patience gives us the best chance of effecting unity and peace, resulting in greater productivity, more honesty, and deeper commitment.

Back to Grenny. In his view the goal of crucial conversations is to use them as "trust-building accelerants that improve the core of families and organizations, thus affecting everything else." In other words, the goal of dialogue is to channel the energy of conflict in a win/win direction.

As to the means of achieving this goal, Grenny writes that masters of dialogue create an atmosphere where all the parties feel safe adding their own views, no matter how controversial, to the "shared pool" of ideas being expressed. Creating this pool, according to Grenny, will require patience, "but," he notes, "the outcome will be more valuable."

There are, Grenny adds, two essential safety conditions for any dialogue, "purpose" and "respect." If others become convinced of our malicious intent or lack of respect, they will almost certainly react in anger, ending all meaningful dialogue. To restore free flowing meaning, Grenny advocates a response that communicates our willingness to listen to their concerns (gentleness) and an apology that emphasizes our fundamental respect (humility).

It seems that Grenny and his three coauthors are aligned perfectly with the wisdom of the ages. Maybe that's why folks have found "Crucial Conversations" so helpful that over two million copies have sold.

...listens deeply

Essay 11: Listening Gray

"He who answers before listening–that is his folly and his shame"–Proverbs 18:13

In his 2002 best-selling book "The Contrarian's Guide to Leadership," former University of Southern California president Steven Sample observes that the average person suffers from the delusion that he's a good listener. "Most people, however, including many leaders," Sample writes, "are terrible listeners; they think talking is more important than listening. But [effective] leaders know it is better to listen first and talk later." He suggests not only that we make the effort to listen, but also that we do so "artfully," practicing what he calls "listening gray."

Sample describes listening gray as taking in information and suspending judgment about whether it's true or not for as long as possible. If delaying decisions until the eleventh hour seems counterintuitive, that's because, according to Sample, it is. Most of us, he says, tend to take what he calls a binary approach to listening and thinking: when we hear something, we are inclined to categorize it immediately as good or bad, true or false, black or white. To suspend judgment demands a concerted effort.

But then thinking gray is also counterintuitive because our stereotypical view of great leaders–probably driven by Hollywood – tends to be that because they are passionate, opinionated individuals they by nature make instant decisions. Can you imagine Gen. George Patton, with his reputation for rapid and aggressive offensive action, thinking gray? Well, yes, actually. Most noted military leaders, Sample points out, know "the value of suspending judgment about important matters, and especially about the validity of incoming intelligence, until the last possible moment."

Sample contends that binary thinking hinders leadership because it closes our mind to hear and process subsequent information that could make all the difference in arriving at the best decision.

So how does one cultivate this unnatural ability to suspend judgment in order to listen deeply to another's point of view? I remember attending some years ago a luncheon presentation by Don Hayes. A former president of GTE Data Services, Inc., Hayes had had responsibility for 6,000 employees and a billion-dollar budget. In his remarks that day Hayes recounted a personal anecdote about listening. His story so impressed me that I transcribed verbatim from the recording that portion of his comments. Here's what he said:

"I used to go into meetings as the leader of a large organization, and I knew what the outcome was going to be: I was going to fight and make it happen the way I thought it should. You don't get to where I was by being a milquetoast. But I learned that I could go into that meeting and while these hard discussions were going on, I could be praying: 'Lord, just help me understand this. Give me wisdom. Let me hear what these other people are saying.'

"I discovered that coming out of those meetings the decisions weren't radically different than what I went in thinking, but they had moved a little bit. And that little bit of movement made it a better decision than if I had just ramrodded the thing through. I found myself able to listen to people more and not having to be such a control freak."

Sample notes in his book that with many leaders, the higher the level they reach, the worse listeners they become. Seeing themselves primarily as order givers, as Hayes once did, they fail to value the opinion of subordinates. What Don described was for him the practical outworking of his decision to open his life to Jesus Christ through faith. God was now helping shape his perspective. A new appreciation for others resulted in his efforts to draw out their viewpoints, i.e., to listen gray. It made him a better leader.

...transcends self

Essay 12: Beware of a Shadow Mission

"Those who will not be moved from doing right will live, but those who pursue evil will bring about their own death" – Proverbs 11:19

*What is a leader's greatest fear? Failure? Mutiny? Criticism? All are possibilities, but I would suggest that the leader's greatest fear is, or ought to be, not something that we do, which is recoverable, but something that can happen inside us. Let me explain.

Jim Collins in his monumental book, "Good to Great," describes several characteristics of CEO's who took their companies to the highest level of excellence. He calls these rare individuals "Level 5 Leaders." Collins' research revealed that Level 5 leaders "are ambitious, to be sure, but ambitious first and foremost for the company, not themselves...Level 5 leaders display a compelling modesty, are self-effacing and understated..." We might well conclude that exhibiting these qualities is a leader's true mission.

But we've seen enough "Bernie" Madoffs and Lance Armstrongs to know that not all leaders embrace a mission of humility and sacrifice. The fact is it's quite easy for our life as leaders to deteriorate into something self-centered and dark–a "shadow mission" if you will. The ancient Hebrew scriptures tell us that this kind of thing has been going on since Adam and Eve bought the line to eat from the tree and become like God. My contention is that we all are tempted daily to center our life around something unworthy and dark.

The Bible book of "Esther" offers insights into this choice leaders make between true and shadow missions. The principal players in the story are the Persian king, Xerxes; Haman, Xerxes' chief of staff; Esther, a beautiful Jewish orphan girl; and Esther's cousin Mordecai, who adopted and raised her.

As the curtain on this drama rises, Esther becomes Xerxes' queen by winning a beauty contest. Her shadow mission is to be eye candy for the king. All goes well until Haman, driven by his shadow mission to destroy Mordecai, the one man who will not bow down and give him worship, offers the king a bribe to decree the destruction of Mordecai and all the Jews throughout the Persian Empire. Xerxes, preoccupied with his own shadow mission to show off his greatness and unaware, as Haman is, that Esther is Jewish, grants Haman's request.

When word of this reaches Mordecai, he quickly realizes that only Esther is in a position to save Israel, and he charges her to go to the king and plead for their lives. She balks. It's a capital offense to approach the king unsummoned, unless he extends the golden scepter. And Xerxes hasn't summoned Esther for thirty days.

But Mordecai presses (paraphrase): "You have not been brought to this point for some shadow mission of selfishly enjoying fame and security. Your true mission is to work for justice and to spare your people great suffering."

Facing one of the great challenges of leadership, Esther calls on Mordecai to arrange for their people to join her in three days of fasting and prayer. To try to achieve this mission she will not rely on her beauty and cleverness alone. On the third day, she tells Mordecai, "I will go to the king, and if I perish, I perish."

Because Esther courageously says no to the shadow mission of luxury and security and yes to her true mission,

Haman ends up hanging from the noose he intended for Mordecai, Mordecai becomes Xerxes' chief of staff in Haman's place and writes a new edict that saves Israel, and the people who marked the Jews for death are themselves destroyed.

What is a leader's greatest fear? I believe it ought to be that instead of sacrificing and serving, we might go after a selfish shadow mission and in so doing inflict harm rather than bestow benefit on both the organization and the people.

A couple insights from "Esther": One, courage in going after the true mission is indispensible, and in partnership with God we'll have more courage to go farther beyond self than otherwise. Two, it's a good idea to have a Mordecai around to encourage us to the task.

*Adapted from remarks by John Ortberg titled "A Leader's Greatest Fear"

...holds fast to convictions

Essay 13: Authentic Leadership

"The evil man gets rich for the moment, but the good man's reward lasts forever" – Proverbs 11:18

In "Leadership Lessons from West Point," a collection of essays published by The Leader to Leader Institute, Lt. Col. Sean Hannah, at the time Director of leadership and management studies for the Department of Behavioral Sciences and Leadership at West Point, writes, "Authentic leadership occurs when followers idealize their leader and internalize the leader's vision and ideals."

Continuing in the chapter "The Authentic High-Impact Leader," Hannah's contribution to this anthology, the Colonel notes that: "Through the hands-on leadership opportunities and challenges I have experienced in two decades of Army leadership and reinforced through research as a leadership scholar, one primary tenet has consistently emerged: at its core, true leadership stems from the leader's authenticity."

Hannah defines authenticity as holding to one's moral convictions despite being constantly challenged by one's environment and the expectations of others to betray one's values. Individuals who exhibit this quality, he observes, enjoy far greater power and influence in their leadership than the leader who bases his power on his position, doling out rewards and punishments to gain compliance.

In support of Dr. Hannah's thesis I offer as "Exhibit A" Moses, the former Egyptian prince later turned prophet, religious leader and lawgiver, who delivered his people from enslavement in Egypt. I propose for your consideration that it was Moses' authenticity that made him one of history's foremost leaders.

The New Testament book of Hebrews, serving as sort of a commentary on Moses' experience in Egypt, records that although born a Hebrew slave, Moses was raised as the grandson of Pharaoh, the world's most powerful man. At 40, we're told, Moses faced an identity crisis. He had to decide, "Am I a Hebrew or am I an Egyptian? Am I a slave or am I royalty?" To put it another way, he had to settle the issue, "What are my values for life? What am I living for?"

Good question. What are your and my values for life? Someone has observed that it's critical to have a value system of our own since, if we fail to decide what's important in our life, our culture will gladly project its value system on us.

And what is our culture's value system? Well, certainly it has to do with prestige, pleasure and possessions. In our world fame always brings a certain amount of honor. If we're born into the right family or we're a successful athlete or entertainer, we're thought of us as great, whether we are or not. If we have money, regardless of how we got it, the world will hold us in high esteem. If we have enough degrees behind our name, certain people will think we have arrived. The same is true of political power, etc.

Ironically, as an Egyptian, Moses had most of these things. Yet, Hebrews informs us that after considering what was important to him and what wasn't, he elected to walk away from all of this to cast his lot with the Israelites. Talk about refusing to betray one's values in spite of the challenges of environment and expectations! That, my friends, is authenticity. Little wonder Moses enjoyed such influence. Who of us wouldn't follow a leader like that, someone we could trust to say what he means and do what he says?

By the way, what motivated Moses to make such an uncompromising choice? Hebrews explains that he was looking forward to a great reward. In keeping with the principle outlined in Proverbs 11:18, Moses recognized that the culture's values, while pleasurable, are fleeting, while the rewards of the good man, the individual who buys into God's value system, will endure forever. So Moses organized his priorities accordingly. How about you and me?

...learns eagerly from all

Essay 14: A Janitor's Lesson in Leadership

"He who oppresses the poor shows contempt for their Maker, but whoever is kind to the needy honors God" – Proverbs 14:31

Jim Moschgat, in the late 70s a cadet at the Air Force Academy, one of the nation's premier leadership laboratories, tells the story of their squadron janitor, William "Bill" Crawford (Colonel Moschgat's article is available at www.homeofheroes.com/profiles/profiles_crawford_10lessons.html).

Although Crawford kept the place spotless, says Moschgat, none of the cadets gave him much notice, "rendering him little more than a passing nod or throwing a curt, 'G'morning!' in his direction as we hurried off to our daily duties.... Face it, Bill was an old man working in a young person's world. What did he have to offer us on a personal level?"

One Saturday, however, Moschgat "stumbled across an incredible story" while reading a book about World War II. It was the account of how in September 1943, on Hill 424 near Altavilla, Italy, a Private William Crawford, "in the face of intense and overwhelming hostile fire ... with no regard for personal safety ... on his own initiative, single-handedly attacked fortified enemy positions." It continued, "For conspicuous gallantry and intrepidity at risk of life above and beyond the call of duty, the President of the United States ..."

Moschgat knew that Bill Crawford, janitor, was a WWII Army vet, but could it be that this man who "quietly moved about the squadron mopping and buffing floors, emptying trash cans, and cleaning toilets" was a winner of the Congressional Medal of Honor, the nation's highest award for gallantry? Surely not, Moschgat thought.

Bright and early on Monday Moschgat met Crawford and showed him the page in question from the book. "He stared at it for a few silent moments and then quietly uttered something like, 'Yep, that's me.' 'Why didn't you ever tell us about it?'" Crawford stuttered. "He slowly replied after some thought, 'That was one day in my life, and it happened a long time ago.'"

"Word spread like wildfire among the cadets that we had a hero in our midst," writes Moschgat. "Cadets who had once passed by Bill with hardly a glance, now greeted him with a smile and a respectful, 'Good morning, Mr. Crawford'.... Almost overnight, Bill went from being a simple fixture in our squadron to one of our teammates.... He even got to know most of us by our first names, something that didn't happen often at the Academy."

Moschgat draws a number of insightful leadership lessons from his experience with Bill Crawford, janitor, one of which is, "All too often, we look to some school to teach us about leadership when, in fact, life is a leadership laboratory. Those you meet everyday will teach you enduring lessons if you just take time to stop, look and 'listen.' I spent four years at the Air Force Academy, took dozens of classes, read hundreds of books, and met thousands of great people. I gleaned leadership skills from all of them, but one of the people I remember most is Mr. Bill Crawford and the lessons he unknowingly taught. Don't miss your opportunity to learn."

Thanks to Colonel Jim Moschgat for this illustration of Proverbs 14:31, which points to the inherent worth in every person. The truly wise understand this truth and eagerly look to learn from everyone, including those that some deem lowly and insignificant.

...connects authentically

Essay 15: Engaging with Those We Lead

"A servant cannot be corrected by mere words; though he understands, he will not respond" – Proverbs 29:19

Why is it that some leaders can capture their people's best efforts while others get only compliance? In his book "Integrity," psychologist and business consultant Henry Cloud maintains that engaging others' will is a function of the leader's character.

When we think of "character" or "integrity," usually we have in mind ethics and morals. But Cloud argues that integrity has a broader meaning than being honest.

He points out that the "Oxford Dictionary" defines "integrity" as the quality of being honest, but also as the state of being unified, whole, undivided. Cloud: "When we are talking about integrity, we are talking about being a whole person, an integrated person, with all of our different parts delivering the functions that they were designed to deliver." Following this definition, Cloud asserts that the most effective leaders are not just ethical, but also have other aspects of integrity, i.e. they are "running on all cylinders," which enables them to be successful.

One of the "other" aspects of integrity, according to Cloud, is the ability to engage with people, to connect authentically with them. To illustrate, he cites the example of a CEO who took over a new company formed from the merger of two companies. This CEO was full of positive energy and great with numbers. In addition, he was a "nice guy."

When the CEO addressed the management teams of both companies for the first time, Cloud, who attended the meeting as a consultant, writes that the CEO did well as long as he talked about the analysis of the industry and the opportunities created by a changing world. But when he ended his presentation and took questions, "it all fell apart."

One after another, the managers expressed deep concern about layoffs, employee benefits, and merging the two cultures. In each case, Cloud notes, the CEO's response failed to connect with the people's apprehensions. Instead of identifying with his managers' feelings in a way that let them know he had heard their hearts, he told them why their concerns were unjustified.

Proverbs 29:19 stresses that in developing an organization's most valuable resource, facts and figures just won't do the job unless they're backed up with relationships. Cloud's observation is that although the CEO was talented, competent and a nice guy, because he lacked integrity – i.e., he wasn't "unified, whole, undivided"–he was unable to establish a heartfelt connection with his people. In turned out that in less than a year the CEO was gone.

In Cloud's judgment this leader did not possess the ingredient most essential to engaging others, "empathy." "He did not help the people see that he could be in their... shoes. And if we don't feel that someone knows what it is like to be us, what they say has little credibility."

Why do some struggle to empathize with others? Detachment. Cloud: "Connection is the opposite of 'detachment,' whereby a person is a kind of island to him- or herself.... Detachment is about not crossing the space to actually enter into another person's world... Sadly, a lot of loving and nice people are detached in this way, and their relationships suffer for it."

Overcoming detachment begins with (Cloud:) "seeing and caring about another person's heart." The scriptures put it this way: "Each of you should look not only to your own interests, but also to the interests of others." And God promises to answer our appeals for help in pulling this off.

When as leaders we have the character to get out of ourselves long enough to know and value others, the reward is great, whether in business, marriage, friendship, or parenting. Instead of just pulling others along, there is an energy, says Cloud, that we feel that is the natural by-product of connectedness. "It is the 'life force' that fuels all sorts of drive, passion, and accomplishment in every aspect of life."*

*In addition to Cloud's book, the YouTube video, "Employee Engagement – Who's Sinking Your Boat?" is an excellent resource on this topic.

...pursues wisdom persistently

Essay 16: Wisdom & Influence

"I, wisdom, dwell together with prudence; I possess knowledge and discretion. By me kings reign and rulers make laws that are just" – Proverbs 8:12,15

My favorite definition of "leadership" is John Maxwell's. In "The 21 Irrefutable Laws of Leadership" Maxwell writes, "The true meaning of leadership is influence – nothing more, nothing less."

I like that. One reason is it's easy to remember. But it's also true.

Of course, influence isn't always about leadership. If an elephant breaks into a room, no one can argue that the pachyderm doesn't have influence, but he's not a leader. So, not everything that has influence is a leader, but all real leaders have influence. Without influence it's not possible to lead.

Influence – again, Maxwell–is what distinguishes leaders from managers. Managers, he notes, can maintain direction, but can't change it. Leaders move people in a new direction, and for that, influence is required.

How does one develop influence? You ever been put in a position where you needed to lead but you lacked influence? Speaking from experience, that's sort of like being handed a set of reins only to discover that they're not connected to anything. So how does one develop influence?

We'd all agree that influence is a product of position, intelligence, knowledge, relationships and a number of other similar elements that we must cultivate and capitalize on if we're to have influence. But I'd like to suggest another factor, maybe not as obvious as the others, that bears on influence and hence on leadership, as much as, maybe more than, any other.

You may be familiar with the Bible book of Ecclesiastes. Sort of a commentary written by Israel's King Solomon after an exhaustive study of what gives life meaning, one of Solomon's conclusions is, "Wisdom makes one wise man more powerful [read, 'influential'] than ten rulers in a city." Solomon says you take the mayor, the CEOs of the biggest corporations in town, you throw in a couple other local powerbrokers, and you stack all these "rulers" up against somebody with wisdom, and the wise guy has more influence.

A "for instance" is Solomon himself. Given the gift of wisdom by God, according to the scriptures, when Solomon was the newly crowned king of Israel, he faced a conundrum. Two new moms, both prostitutes–one of whom, likely in a drunken stupor, had suffocated her newborn–appeared before Solomon claiming to be the mother of the living child. With deep insight into basic human nature Solomon cracked the case (see how in 1 Kings 3). The text reports that when word of how Solomon's wisdom had enabled him to understand how people behave in various situations, his subjects "held him in awe." That's influence.

Then there were the advisors to Israel's King David identified simply as the men of Issachar. 2 Chronicles tells us that these fellows "knew the times and understood what Israel should do." What kind of influence do you suppose a group of folks with wisdom enough to unscrew America's inscrutable problems would wield today?

In the Bible book of Acts, Saint Paul, prisoner on a boat with 275 others, including crew and Roman guards, in a storm-tossed sea that threatens to break the ship apart becomes the most influential man on the boat. Why? Based on wisdom he had confidence in God that enabled him to keep his head when around him all others were losing theirs.

If we agree that wisdom significantly enhances our leadership effectiveness, as leaders we ought to be interested in how one becomes wise. The Bible tells us that only God can give the kind of wisdom that marked Solomon, the men of Issachar, and Saint Paul. The good news of the ancient text is that this sort of wisdom is available to anyone willing to prayerfully and diligently search the scriptures for it.

...sacrifices willingly

Essay 17: Jesus' "Level 5" Leader

"Love and faithfulness form a good leader; sound leadership is founded on loving integrity"–Proverbs 20:28

What is the DNA of a true leader? Many would say it's the ability to achieve results. In marketplace parlance that usually means beating analysts' projections for quarterly earnings.

Lee Iacocca, for instance. As CEO of Chrysler in the 80s he masterminded one of the most celebrated business turnarounds ever. Under his direction Chrysler rose from near bankruptcy to a height of 2.9 times the market at a point about halfway through his tenure. But then Iacocca fixated on making himself a celebrity. He appeared regularly on talk shows, personally starred in over 80 commercials and widely promoted his autobiography, which sold seven million copies and elevated him to rock star status. His personal stock soared, but in the second half of his tenure, Chrysler's stock fell 31 percent behind the general market.

When Iacocca retired, Chrysler experienced a brief return to glory for the next five years, but then, according to Jim Collins' blockbuster book "Good to Great," "the company's

underlying weaknesses led to a buyout by Daimler-Benz...
[marking] the demise of Chrysler as a stand-alone company."

Iacocca's story is one of several that Collins cites to illustrate his point that boards of directors frequently operate
under the misconception that they need to hire a larger-
than-life, ego centric leader to make the organization great.
As a result what they often end up with is someone whose
arrogance and abuse of power wreak havoc.

Contrary to this conventional wisdom, Collins' research
found that the CEOs who took good organizations and turned
them into great ones ("Level 5 leaders") were humble and
modest. Interestingly, 2,000 years ago Jesus, regarded by
many as history's foremost leader, modeled and taught a
similar, but I would argue, distinctly different leadership
paradigm, one he described as "servant leadership."

The difference between Collins' Level 5 leader and Jesus'
leadership model is reflected in the "violent" objection of
Collins' research team to the term "servant leader" to char-
acterize Level 5 leaders. To Collins' team, attaching the label
"servant leaders" to those who "will sell the mills or fire their
brother, if that's what it takes to make the company great,"
made them sound "weak and meek." The data led the team
to conclude that what distinguished Level 5 leaders as a
group was not necessarily their concern for others' welfare,
but their passion to make the company great.

In Jesus' model leadership is about serving. Period.
In Matthew 20, for example, Jesus instructs his followers,
"You know that the rulers in this world lord it over their
people.... But among you it will be different. Whoever wants
to become great among you must be your servant, and whoever wants to be first among you must become your slave."
Jesus spoke here of a level of leadership that goes beyond
great to "greatest," a level reserved for the leader whose
commitment to use his resources to serve others is unre-
served. A few days later, Jesus provided an unforgettable

example of this supreme level of leadership by laying down his life to redeem mankind.

Collins' Level 5 leader is leader first. He may well serve his employees, but he does so out of his ambition to create and sustain a great company. In Jesus' leadership paradigm, a "Level 5 leader" is servant first; by building people into greatness he creates "the greatest" organization. [Note: How "great" was Jesus' "organization"? Within a few years of his death his enemies grudgingly acknowledged that his followers had "turned the world upside down."]

Very simply, the difference between these two leadership models, in keeping with Proverb 20:28, is that Jesus' model is love-driven. No question, people can be empowered to excellence by humble and modest leaders that are performance-driven, but I would argue that our highest level of performance is reserved for beyond-great leaders like Jesus, leaders who, motivated by love, willingly sacrifice for other's welfare.

Category 2

Whoever goes hunting for what is right and kind finds life itself – <u>glorious</u> life! – King Solomon (Proverbs 21:21)

Essays 18-37:

Living with excellence results from...

...doing what's right and good

Essay 18: A Life Well Lived

A life well lived is the theme of an ad campaign promoting San Miguel, a Spanish beer. Such a life, the unseen narrator tells us in a made for TV ad, is about experiences of beauty, romance, mischief and adventure, including being rescued by an admiral's daughter and being swallowed whole by a fish.

To which I say, not so fast. Celebrated author Ernest Hemingway lived an intrepid life. A foreign correspondent in both World Wars who also traveled extensively in pursuit of hunting and other sports, Hemingway had wide-ranging experiences. However, at age 61, lonely, suffering from paranoia and plagued by a variety of physical problems aggravated by years of heavy alcohol consumption, Hemingway's legendary life of adventure, flamboyance and celebrity ended by his own hand.

For others, a life well lived is about success. The story is told of a businessman who was at the pier of a small coastal

Mexican village when a small boat with just one fisherman docked. Inside the boat were several large yellowfin tuna. The businessman complimented the Mexican on his fish and asked how long it took to catch them. "Only a little while," the Mexican replied. The businessman then asked why he didn't stay out longer and catch more fish. The Mexican said he had enough to support his family's immediate needs. The businessman then asked, "But what do you do with the rest of your time?" "Well, señor," the Mexican fisherman said, "I sleep late, fish a little, play with my children, take a siesta with my wife, and stroll into the village every evening where I sip wine and play guitar with my amigos."

The businessman scoffed. "You should spend more time fishing and with the proceeds buy a bigger boat, then a fleet of boats. Instead of selling your catch to a middleman, you could sell directly to the processor and eventually open your own cannery. You would of course need to move to Mexico City, then to LA and eventually to New York City where you would run your expanding enterprise."

The Mexican fisherman asked, "But how long will this all take?" To which the businessman replied, "15-20 years." "But what then, señor?" The businessman laughed and said, "That's the best part! When the time is right, you sell your company and become rich." "Then what, señor?" "Then you would retire," said the businessman, "and move to a small coastal fishing village where you would sleep late, fish a little, play with your kids, take a siesta with your wife, stroll to the village in the evenings where you could sip wine and play your guitar with your amigos." Smiling, the fisherman said, "Isn't that what I'm doing right now?"

Clearly the Mexican angler was closer to solving the "What is a life well lived?" riddle than the business guy. But for a more complete answer yet, I suggest we consider what the incomparably wise King Solomon wrote on this topic.

If a life well lived is about joy, courage, peace and honor, then Solomon regarded such a life as the natural result of living righteously, i.e., doing what is right and good. For instance, he says in Proverbs, "The life of the righteous is full of light and joy" (13:9); "The righteous are bold as a lion" (28:1); "When people's lives please the Lord, even their enemies are at peace with them" (16:7); "He who pursues righteousness and love finds life, prosperity and honor" (21:21).

So it turns out that while living a good and honest life may in some quarters be considered a bit dull and too conventional, it does have substantial advantages according to the best selling book of all time (and perhaps a certain Mexican fisherman).

...winning others' respect

Essay 19: Making a Good Name

What's the value of a good name? Would you believe it's virtually priceless? So says the Bible book of Proverbs: "A good name is more desirable than great riches; to be esteemed is better than silver or gold" (22:1).

Nowadays one can do just about anything to make a name for himself. Here are a few quotes from folks who made a name for themselves. See how many you recognize. "I never felt like I was cheating" – Lance Armstrong when asked about his use of performance enhancing drugs. "It's a proprietary strategy. I can't go into it in great detail"–Bernie Madoff. "I feel empowered when I see myself in a T-shirt" – Miley Cyrus. Making a name for ourselves is easy, but what kind of name are we making?

Any idea what the Bible says is key to winning the respect of others? Here are three things. One, Proverbs 17:7

observes, "Respected people do not tell lies..." Few things undermine a man's reputation as fast as fraud or lying. Respect is won though integrity. Granted, honesty may not always be popular in the corporate boardroom, particularly in companies whose only code of ethics is how will it play out in the media. And for the entrepreneur, unvarnished truth may sometimes shrink his bottom line. But we're talking here about how to have a good name, which, according to the Bible, is "more desirable than great riches."

Integrity, then, is essential to a good name. So is humility. Proverbs 29:23 reminds us that "a man's pride brings him low." Did you hear about the minister who was doing this wedding? He's waxing eloquent–I mean, people are hanging on his every word–and he starts thinking, "Hey, I really am doing pretty good today." And pride begins to well up in the reverend. Then all of a sudden he notices that his fly is unzipped.

"Not a problem for someone as slick as I am," he thinks. "I'll just zip up during the prayer." So he says, "Shall we pray?" As they bow, he zips up...and catches the bride's dress in his zipper. Now he's praying about everything he can think of while working frantically, and unsuccessfully, to clear his zipper. Finally, he says, "Amen," and he goes, "May I present to you Mr. and Mrs. Smith." Then he puts his arm around the couple and whispers, "Just keep walking," and he follows them out of the chapel.

Most of us think intuitively, "If I don't hide my weaknesses and pretend I've got it all together, people won't respect me." But you and I know from experience that the more people are willing to own their foul ups and limitations, the more highly we tend to regard them. Humility is indispensable to a good name.

And so is spirituality. Proverbs 3:4-6 asserts that those who "trust in the Lord," rather than simply relying on their own perceptions, "win favor and a good name in the sight of God and man." Now if the mention of spirituality conjures up for you thoughts of a sentimental, syrupy kind of religiosity, that's not what he's talking about here. The spirituality of Proverbs 3 describes somebody genuinely devoted to God who puts God first in his life. Folks are drawn to that. Take recently retired Yankee closer Mariano Rivera for instance. He was one of the most admired men in all of sports, respected for his lifestyle even by those who don't share his faith.

So what will people say about you and me when we're gone? I want to be remembered by my kids, grandkids and maybe a few others as a man who was respected because I told the truth, had a humble opinion of myself and loved God. What about you?

...reflecting wisdom in decisions

Essay 20: The Decisions You Make, Make You

"The Proverbs of Solomon...for attaining wisdom and discipline; for understanding words of insight; for acquiring a disciplined and prudent life" – Proverbs 1:1-3

I agree with leadership expert John Maxwell when he says that each of us is where we are today because of decisions we've already made, and that the decisions we make today will determine where we'll be tomorrow.

As I approach 70, I have several goals that for me equate to finishing well, making the most of the remainder of my life. I recognize, however, that none of these goals will materialize without me making several value decisions.

It occurs to me that our value decisions are based on either wisdom or foolhardiness, with a result that is either honorable ("prudent") or shameful. Israel's king Solomon made both types of decisions and experienced both results. Fortunately, the wisdom principles Solomon learned from his experiences he recorded in the book of Proverbs (see verses above).

Much of what follows is from "Decisions That Have Shaped My Life," a presentation by John Maxwell in which he describes several key decisions he made that resulted in him becoming who he is today. Because Maxwell's decisions reflect wisdom from Proverbs, I'm using his remarks as a guide to making key decisions that I'm persuaded will help me finish well. This essay may also help you in your decision-making. That's my hope.

Maxwell attributes much of his success to his decision to develop his strengths everyday. We all have strength and limitations. There are things we do well, which, with concentrated effort, we can do even better. There are also things we don't do well, which, no matter how much effort we put into, we'll never be good at. Maxwell's counsel is to pinpoint our natural abilities and then determine to work everyday to strengthen them. ("Do you see someone skilled in their work? They will serve before kings" – Proverbs 22:29.)

Essential to the development of our strengths, Maxwell maintains, is our environment. He says it's a decision to hang around people who are ahead of us, who are themselves growing, who challenge us to get out of our comfort zone that will help us keep growing.

A second life-shaping decision for Maxwell was his choice to help others get what they need so that they in turn will help him get what he needs. ("As iron sharpens iron, so one man sharpens another" – Proverbs 27:17.)

There are ladder climbers, people who say, "How can I make myself more successful?" and there are ladder builders, those whose motto is, "How can I make others more successful?" The climber goes fast because he goes alone, but it's the builder who goes far because he goes together. Whose needs are you and I focused on, ours or others'? We all have a choice.

Maxwell's third key decision, this one just for people of faith, is to choose to attempt things so big that, if accomplished, only God will get the credit. ("Trust in the Lord with all your heart...and he will make your paths straight"– Proverbs 3:5-6.)

Thirty-five years ago, Dr. Bill Bright, founder of the organization that I'm on staff with, produced the "Jesus" film out of his vision to reach each person, and every people, in their heart language, with the good news of Jesus Christ. This film has now been dubbed in some 1300 languages and over 200 million people in 220 countries have come to know Christ through this project. That's big!

Maxwell: "There are times when leaders feel obligated to talk farther than they have walked. At those times they don't feel holy enough, strong enough, or qualified enough. It is at that time that they should allow their weaknesses to bring them to God who is MORE than enough!" I'm convinced that for me to finish well means to choose to reject the temptation to "stack arms" and coast and instead decide to attempt things so big that if accomplished only God will get the credit. How about you?

...remembering that life is fleeting

Essay 21: Making the Most of Life

Chances are pretty good I know something about you even though we've probably never met: you're committed to making the most of your life. Why else would you be reading this essay?

Now there's no shortage of suggestions on ways to leverage our influence: assemble the right credentials; choose a career that fits our strengths; cultivate a network of interesting acquaintances and friends; etc. To these excellent ideas allow me to add another, drawn from the pages of scripture and perhaps less familiar to you.

I invite your attention to Proverbs 27:1, which offers this bit of counsel: "Do not boast about tomorrow, for you do not know what a day may bring forth."

Because the future is largely beyond our control Solomon warns here against presuming on tomorrow, as we do, for instance, when we procrastinate. Who of us has never had intentions to tell a family member how proud we are of them, or encourage a friend in crisis, or repair a damaged relationship by apologizing, but we didn't because we thought, "I'll do that later"? That's boasting about tomorrow, and it prevents us from making the most of our life.

Solomon's words here are intended to exhort us, in light of tomorrow's uncertainty, to capitalize on today. This idea was driven home to me in a memorable way around the time of my 45th high school reunion. Have you ever found yourself at an event with folks mostly your age, and at some point you look around and think, "What are all these older people doing here?" At that reunion I experienced that kind of unsettling awareness of my advancing age.

That same weekend there was also a subtle, recurring reminder that for all of us death closes the circle of life. A DVD was shown in memory of a classmate killed years ago in Vietnam. We also learned the sad news of the passing of other members of our class or their spouse.

Then, a couple days following the reunion, I read of the death of a close friend who lived in another state. I was aware that Rick, a few years younger than I, was suffering from a serious heart condition. Still, the word of his fatal attack was a shock.

Finally, a day or two later, the news came of the passing of another friend, a fellow West Point graduate about my age. Terry and I had developed a friendship in the 70s during the five years that we worked for the same company. Again, a jolt. My mind's eye envisioned a young man in his 20s, full of life and ambition.

It occurred to me at the time that through these events God was reminding me, "Jim, I have a good plan for your life, but remember that you have a limited opportunity to execute it." It was as though he was saying to me, "Don't boast about tomorrow; don't procrastinate."

The Bible records that Israel's King David was an outstanding chief of state, a world-class poet and musician, the religious "bishop" of a nation, and an unparalleled military commander. So wide-ranging were David's achievements that one author calls his "the most successful royal career recorded in the annals of history." How was David able to pour so much into one life? His words in Psalm 39 give insight: "Show me, O Lord, my life's end and the number of my days; let me know how fleeting is my life.... But now, Lord, what do I look for? My hope is in you."

David says here, "God, keep me aware that life is short, so that, with your help, I may make the most of it." I've found praying this prayer helpful to maximizing my own life, and I recommend it to you.

...acting out the Christian ethic

Essay 22: Why So Much Hypocrisy among Christians?

After his experiences with apartheid and "Christians" during his time in South Africa, Mahatma Gandhi is reported to have said, "I like your Christ; I do not like your Christians. Your Christians are so unlike your Christ."

In preparation for writing his revealing book "Unchristian," David Kinnaman studied the values and lifestyles of "born-again" Christians versus non-born-again adults. He found that while born-agains owned more Bibles, attended church more often, and donated money to religious nonprofits (especially to a church), in the matter of daily actions and attitudes, there was little difference between born-agains and non-born-agains.

Concurrent with Kinnaman's study a survey was done of people who considered themselves outside the Christian faith, but who were personally acquainted with at least one "Christian." Of those questioned only 15% said that the life-style of the Christians they knew was any different from the norm. In other words, most "unbelievers" view "believers" as hypocrites.

It's true that too often we who claim to be born again behave contrary to our stated convictions. On the other hand, it's equally true that many have experienced dramatic change through connection with Jesus. To name a couple, John Newton morphed from slave-trader into beloved pastor and author of "Amazing Grace," and Chuck Colson, former Nixon Whitehouse "hatchet man," started an organization that offers hope through faith in Christ to prisoners around the world. I would argue that there is abundant evidence to support the contention that there's something to this Christian "thing." But why so much hypocrisy?

Proverbs 14:26 explains: "Reverence for God gives a man deep strength." God's power, he says, is available to us, but only if we reverence him. In other words, not everyone, not even every born-again Christian, can draw on God's power for right living. He releases it only to those who come to him in love, trust and worship.

St Paul writes about this in Romans. He says, I agree that God's moral code is holy and good, but, even though I have been born again, because old habits die hard, sometimes I choose to do wrong. Who, he asks, will rescue me from this dilemma? His answer: "God does this through our Lord Jesus Christ!" Freedom from old habits, Paul explains, comes through the power God gives to those who approach him as "Lord."

Born again or not, if we depend on human willpower alone, we will cave in the face of some temptations. To act out the Christian ethic requires God's help, which he gives only to those devoted to him. Because most Christians ebb and flow in our devotion, we sometimes fall into hypocrisy.

According to a study entitled, "The Ethics of American Youth," when professing Christian youth and non-Christian youth were asked if in the last 12 months they had physically hurt someone when angered, lied to a parent or a teacher, or cheated on a test, there was just a 4% difference between the actions of the two groups. Yet, when NBC offered 17-year-old Charity Allen $20,000 a week for five years to play a daytime drama role in which she would become pregnant by a married man, split up his marriage, have an abortion, etc., she turned them down. Why? "I've made Jesus Christ the Lord of my life," she said. "He gave me the strength to do what's right." "Reverence for God gives a man deep strength."

...operating within strengths and passions

Essay 23: The Secret of Success

Do I have a deal for you, today–that is, if you aspire to be successful and fulfilled and to do the very most with your life (which I'm confident that you do). I'm offering without charge advice a career counselor would want a bundle for. This advice has stood the test of time – it's 3000 years old – and it comes from King Solomon, history's wisest man. Here it is, "Do you see a man skilled in his work? He will serve before kings; he will not serve before obscure men" (Proverbs 22:29).

More recently, researchers looking to pinpoint the parameters of success followed the careers of 1500 men and women from age 20 into their 40s. 83 of these 1500 became millionaires. The interesting thing is none of these men and women set out to be wealthy, and none got involved in a get-rich-quick scheme. The secret to their success? They chose a career they loved and became so good at it that people started paying them a lot of money to do it.

That's precisely what Proverbs 22:29 describes. Solomon says, "Find something you love to do, polish that skill until you can do it with excellence, and you're going to be okay." You and I don't have to be good at everything (a plus since we can't be). We just need to find what we're good at, do our best, and forget the rest.

There's this fairytale about how successful people don't have any weaknesses to overcome. Wrong! Malcolm Gladwell wrote a book, "David and Goliath," to show how much of what is beautiful and important in the world comes out of adversity. It's not that successful people don't go through hardship. The difference is they don't let themselves get hung up on it. Instead, they find out what they do well and focus on that.

Researchers Victor and Mildred Goertzel, in a famous study entitled "Cradles of Eminence," looked at the backgrounds of 300 highly successful people, people whose names you'd recognize–Albert Einstein, Franklin Roosevelt, Albert Schweitzer, Helen Keller, Winston Churchill, Mahatma Gandhi, etc.–people who reached the top in their chosen field. The Goertzels studied the home environment of these men and women and discovered that 75% of them as children were troubled either by severe poverty, a broken home, or rejecting, dominating parents. And 25% had some kind of major physical challenge to overcome.

How did these people manage to achieve success in spite of their dysfunctional background? They compensated for their weaknesses by specializing and getting good in an area they loved. The world stands aside for those who know where they're going.

So how do we find out what we're good at? We start by being ourself. Sounds obvious, but most people, instead of being who they are, try to be somebody else, namely, what the culture – i.e., television, "How to Be a Success" seminars and books–says is cool and necessary for success. The irony is that success comes when we're ourself so we can figure out what "our" strengths are.

And here's a really important thing for those of us getting a bit long in the tooth to keep in mind: it's never too late to get this right. We may be into something right now we don't like, but we figure, "I'm too old to change." Oh yeah? At 64, Francis Chichester sailed around the world by himself in a 53-foot yacht. At 72, Golda Meier became the Prime Ministry of Israel. At 73, Grandma Moses decided to start painting, and she gave her first exhibition at 80. At 100, ragtime pianist Eubie Blake exclaimed, "If I'd known I was going to live this long, I'd have taken better care of myself"(!). It's never too late to start doing what God wired us to do.

...developing the mind

Essay 24: Maintaining a Buff Brain

"Those who get wisdom do themselves a favor, and those who love learning will succeed"–Proverbs 19:8.

The Army taught us the value of physical fitness. Even now, though pushing 70, we still jump to conclusions, fly off the handle and put our foot in our mouth. Or is that only me? Anyway, we know the importance of keeping muscles toned and the pulse down. We may not work at it, but we understand the principle.

Proverbs 19:8 spotlights another part of our anatomy that requires regular exercise for peak performance, the little gray cells. It says, "To continue to be successful in life, you've got to keep on learning."

Unfortunately, by the time some folks reach their mid-30s they've stopped developing new skills. The tragedy is that to quit learning is to stop growing and start shrinking. It's sad to see people who gave up thinking 10 or 15 years earlier and now let others do their thinking for them. The proverb reminds us, "Never stop learning; keep on expanding – and not just your waistline – by developing your mind and striving for new insights."

My friend Nick Krawciw, West Point Class of '59, retired from the Army in 1990 after serving 31 years. In recognition of acts of distinguished service too numerous to mention here, both during and after his military career, West Point presented Maj Gen (Ret) Krawciw the 2006 Distinguished Graduate Award.

Nick's credentials are remarkable, but equally impressive (and inspiring) to me over the several years that I've known him personally is his continuing commitment to growing and learning. In areas of his expertise, such as leadership, Nick is still eager to learn from others. What's more, he continues to expand his thinking in new areas. For example, he has become an enthusiastic student of the Christian faith, adding the Christian literature to his wide reading repertoire and speaking at faith events and diligently taking careful notes when others speak.

If you and I are to remain intellectually sharp throughout our life – as Nick has into his late 70s–there are a couple attitudes that the Bible suggests are essential. One is openness – "The intelligent man is always open to new ideas. In fact he looks for them" (Proverbs 18:15). He says openness and mental alertness go hand in hand.

Have you noticed how the willingness to try new things tends to be inversely proportional to age? Who are the folks least likely to embrace new technology? Those of us drawing Social Security. This is the "You can't teach an old dog new tricks" syndrome, often little more than an excuse for a closed mind. Openness to new things and new ways of doing old things is a must for maintaining an incisive mind.

So is humility: "When pride comes, then comes disgrace. But with humility comes wisdom" (Proverbs 11:2). No doubt you're aware that another common hindrance to learning is the idea that, "I already know it all." Hall of Fame basketball coach John Wooden once said, "It's what you learn after you know it all that counts" (emphasis added). He was referring of course to how ego can get in the way of learning.

The human mind is an incredible gift from the Creator. Keeping it in top shape both honors him and pays huge dividends. The more we make maintaining a "buff" brain a top priority, the higher the probability that we'll still be thinking creatively and making a difference well into our 80s, 90s (like my 95-year-old aunt who is in a spelling bee next week!!) and maybe even beyond. "Those who get wisdom do themselves a favor, and those who love learning will succeed."

Essay 25: Who Are the Notes of Our Symphony?

In the 1995 film Mr. Holland's Opus, Richard Dreyfuss plays professional musician Glenn Holland, a man who dreams of one day being a famous conductor. Meanwhile, Mr. Holland takes a job as a high school music teacher. His plan is to complete in his spare time a symphony that he's composing, and move on. As it turns out, however, between demanding teaching and family responsibilities spare time is hard to come by.

As decades pass, Mr. Holland becomes a skilled teacher, using innovative methods to help students understand classical music and inspiring many of them to excel. Yet, when, after 30 years in the classroom, the cancellation of his school's music program leads to early retirement, his symphony still unwritten and believing he's been mostly forgotten by his former students, he wonders if he's accomplished anything in his life.

At a surprise assembly organized in his honor on his final day as a teacher, friends and students, past and present, show him just what he has meant to them. Among those present is Gertrude Lang, a former student who is now sitting governor of the state. Speaking to those gathered she says:

"Mr. Holland had a profound influence on my life and on a lot of lives I know. But I have a feeling that he considers a great part of his own life misspent. Rumor had it he was always working on this symphony of his. And this was going to make him famous, rich, probably both. But Mr. Holland isn't rich and he isn't famous, at least not outside of our little town. So it might be easy for him to think himself a failure. But he would be wrong, because I think that he's achieved a success far beyond riches and fame. Look around you. There is not a life in this room that you have not touched, and each of us is a better person because of you. We are your symphony, Mr. Holland. We are the melodies and the notes of your opus. We are the music of your life."

Question: Who would say that they are the melodies and notes of our symphony?

In the Bible, Proverbs 12:27 tells us, "The lazy man does not roast his game, but the diligent man prizes his possessions." While at first glance this pithy saying that contrasts a hunter too lazy to dress and cook what he's taken in the hunt with a diligent man who values his possessions seems to have little to do with Mr. Holland's story or us, I'd like to suggest that a closer look reveals it has everything to do with both.

Now very near or into our eighth decade, you and I have under our belt a wealth of leadership experiences: the Academy crucible; a career in the military or marketplace or both; community involvement; marriage and family; etc. We've learned much, lots of it through the school of hard knocks, about how life does and doesn't work, about what's true and what has only the appearance of truth, about what brings happiness and what disappoints, about what's worthy of spending life chasing and what isn't. Over the years, whether we recognize it or not, we've acquired insights that many younger people would give their eye-teeth for.

So, whom are you and I mentoring? If it takes a leader to cultivate a leader, whom are we helping to become tomorrow's leaders in the home, church, workplace and nation? The Bible teaches that Jesus had but two primary goals: to redeem mankind and to train 12 leaders to carry on the movement. Whom are we training?

Keeping insights to ourselves that required years and possibly substantial pain to acquire, rather than demonstrating that we prize this possession by doing the work to share it with others, is I think just the sort of thing the above proverb with its hunting metaphor is warning against. Who are the notes of our symphony?

...standing for noble ideals

Essay 26: Memorial Day

"Like the coolness of snow at harvest time is a trustworthy messenger to those who send him..." Proverbs 25:13

Memorial Day dates back to 1868, when May 30th was set aside to honor America's fallen dead of all wars – "trustworthy messengers" sent forth by a not always grateful nation on an errand of mercy, to fight in defense of freedom. I find that, much as an icy drink in the heat of a sweltering day in Oklahoma revitalizes my body, the remembrance of these warriors and their unflagging commitment to duty refreshes my spirit.

Several years ago the Moving Wall, the half-size replica of the Vietnam Veterans Memorial in DC, was exhibited here in Tulsa's Central Park. The Wall is about names, 58,000+ of them. Among these I found "Farl Duane Wagner." Duane and I shared three high school gridiron campaigns. Ironically, the Wall was displayed just a few hundred yards from where the practice field once lay on which in our youth the two of us had sown much sweat and even a little blood while forging our own "band of brothers" bond.

"David Lee Alexander" was also etched into an ebony panel of that tribute to noble sacrifice, as it had been into my memory during the four-year crucible that is West Point. With misty eyes I recalled the passion with which Dave lived ... and how death had snatched him away before his 25th birthday. Duane and Dave, two among that venerable host who, as Stephen Spender wrote, "fought for life...and left the vivid air signed with your honor."

On June 6, 1984, 40 years after the Normandy invasion, President Ronald Reagan spoke at a memorial service above the cliffs at Pointe du Hoc, France. Assembled on that wind-swept promontory in poignant tribute to their fallen comrades were former Rangers whose D-Day objective was to seize the ground where they were now gathered. Following are Mr. Reagan's edited remarks on that solemn occasion:

"At dawn, on the morning of the 6th of June, 1944, 225 Rangers jumped off the British landing craft and ran to the bottom of these cliffs. Their mission was one of the most difficult of the invasion: to climb these sheer and desolate cliffs and take out the enemy guns.

"The Rangers looked up and saw the enemy soldiers–at the edge of the cliff shooting down at them and throwing grenades. And the American Rangers began to climb. They shot rope ladders over the face of these cliffs and began to pull themselves up. When one Ranger fell, another would take his place. When a rope was cut, a Ranger would grab another and begin his climb again. They climbed, shot back, and held their footing. Soon, one by one, the Rangers pulled themselves over the top, and in seizing the firm land at the top of these cliffs, they began to seize back the continent of Europe.

"225 came here. After two days of fighting, only 90 could still bear arms.

"Why? Why did you do it? What impelled you to put aside the instinct for self-preservation and risk your lives to take these cliffs? We look at you and somehow we know the answer. You all knew that some things are worth dying for. One's country is worth dying for, and democracy is worthy dying for, because it is the most deeply honorable form of government ever devised by man.

"Something helped the men of D-Day: the rock-hard belief that Providence would have a hand in what would unfold here, that God would be an ally in this great cause. And so the night before the invasion, when Colonel Wolverton asked his parachute troops to kneel with him in prayer, he told them, 'Do not bow your heads, but look up so you can see God and ask his blessing in what we are about to do.'"

Steeled by the valor of those undaunted Rangers and the countless others, like Duane and Dave, who gave their last full measure of devotion in service to our country, may we, in the words with which President Reagan concluded, "continue to stand for the ideals for which they lived and died."

...maintaining slack

Essay 27: Margin Message from a Matatu

"...when you lie down, your sleep will be sweet...for the Lord will be your confidence..." -- Proverbs 3:24, 26

In his entertaining book The Lunatic Express author Carl Hoffman recounts his hair-raising experiences in Kenya while riding in a form of public transportation known as matatus, privately owned minibuses that Kenya's former president Daniel Arap Moi once called "agents of death and destruction."

Hoffman tells of his matatu drivers honking and flashing their lights in bumper-to-bumper traffic; parrying, jockeying, blocking one another's doors at passenger staging points; jumping curbs onto sidewalks, sending pedestrians scrambling; blasting up Kenya's Ngong Road, an undivided 2-lane strip of cracked blacktop, at speeds up to 100 mph with Bee Gees at deafening volume; leaping off the bus at tea time to wolf down fried dough and sweet tea; paying off cops and inspectors; and chewing mira (a narcotic) to "enhance their alertness on the road" during 18-hour workdays.

While none of us may ever have occasion to decline to ride in a matatu, there is nevertheless a bit of practical wisdom to be gleaned from Hoffman's story. Unless I miss my guess, like most Americans, at times you find yourself, as I do, parrying, jockeying and jumping curbs to gain advantage, or downing a stimulant to enhance alertness while blasting 100 mph down the road of life with Bee Gees at deafening volume. While extreme, the matatu drivers are merely examples of what you and I do, too: live life without margin.

What is margin? Glad you asked. The dictionary says it's the amount available beyond what is really needed; extra; reserve; slack, if you will. In the present context margin is making it to the airport with time to relax and enjoy a Starbucks; marginless is sprinting to make the flight. Margin is taking Saturday as a family day; marginless is working Saturday on business stuff that didn't get done on Friday. Margin is living within our means; marginless is spending all we earn or even more than we earn, as the majority of Americans do.

What happens when our margins disappear? Psychologists tell us that as margin decreases, stress increases. Beyond that, when we live without margin, our relationships go to seed. Are you aware that relationships – with our wife, our children, friends – happen in the margins of life? They do. Busyness is the enemy of closeness.

You and I understand that a good life has margin, and that it's possible to pursue good things to the point that our life is no longer good. Why then don't we simply fix the problem? I don't know. I'm just asking. Could it be we're afraid that we might miss out on something? Perhaps. Bottom line, I believe we're convinced that if we don't live on the edge, somehow our lives won't count. What do you think?

The author of Proverbs 3 reminds us in the verses above that God is calling us away from the edge. In the midst of our fast-paced, highly competitive world, God says if we'll look to him for our confidence, if we'll trust him for our significance instead of measuring our worth by our performance, then we'll be better able to relax, and living with margin will be a whole lot easier.

Funny thing, when because of stress a man suffers a heart attack or a nervous breakdown, all of a sudden he doesn't have any trouble making margin a priority in his life. Wouldn't you agree then that it makes good sense to accept God's help in finding margin now rather than delay and maybe be forced to find it on our own, later?

...deciding correctly about eternity

Essay 28: A No-Brainer Decision!(?)

Did you hear about the two no-good brothers who used their wealth to cover their tracks? They pretended to be upstanding members of the community, both attending the same church.

One of the brothers died suddenly. The day before the funeral the other brother sought out their minister, who was aware of their deception, and handed him a check for a substantial amount.

"There's just one condition," he said. "At his funeral, you have to say my brother was a saint." The minister agreed and deposited the check.

The next day at the funeral, the minister blasted the deceased, branding him a rogue who cheated in business and abused his wife and family. "But," he concluded, "compared to his brother, he was a saint."

Have you noticed how death is sometime the subject of jokes, but almost never a topic of serious discussion. When's the last time you and a friend were enjoying a conversation over a cup of coffee and one of you said, "Let's talk about death"?

We know from experience that in spite of amazing advances in medicine the death rate is still 100%, so why avoid talking about something that's as much a part of life as birth? No doubt it's because death is so final. In spite of what is sometimes said at funeral services, it would seem, based on our observations, that death rings down the curtain on everything we know. How depressing! No wonder we don't like to talk about it.

Fortunately, the Bible offers a different and far more hopeful perspective on death. For instance, Proverbs 14:32 asserts, "The godly have a refuge when they die, but the wicked are crushed by their sins." In the New Testament, Jesus develops this refuge in death idea. By the way, who is better qualified than Jesus to speak about death? Sure, others talk of their experiences while "clinically dead," but a mountain of evidence supports the Bible's claim that Jesus actually died, then came back to tell us what happens after death.

So what does he say? He reports that although death looks like the end, it's not. After death, there's forever, where one of two things happens: One, we celebrate with God with a perfect body, perfect character and perfect circumstances–no more death, dying or pain. Two, we suffer separation–physical, emotional, relational, and spiritual–from God and everything good. In other words, after death there's heaven or there's hell.

Now that's got to be either the greatest good news or the worst bad news, ever. According to Jesus, we get to decide which it is for us.

Does that mean when we die we're going to walk up to St. Peter, and he's going to say, "Which door do you choose?" No, it's not going to be a "Let's Make a Deal" sort of thing. The Bible says – and I'd like to suggest to you that this is really important–that we make the heaven or hell choice right here, on this side of eternity. And it says the choice has to do with Jesus. We either choose him now as savior–our "refuge"–or we face him later as judge (and "are crushed by our sins"). It would seem to be a no-brainer decision!

...choosing the loving thing

Essay 29: The DNA of a Genuine Friend

"A friend loves at all times..."–Proverbs 17:17

In a chapter on "The Discipline of Friendship,"* Kent Hughes writes, "Few men have good friends, much less deep friendships." Hughes notes that America's leading psychologists and therapists estimate that only 10% of all men ever have any real friends.

The problem, Hughes says, stems from the way men are wired. Unlike women, men are more into doing than talking. Because we gear ourselves for the marketplace, we men understand friendships more as acquaintances than as relationships. Adding to our deficiency, Hughes notes, is our bent to buy into the Hollywood delusion that "real men don't need other people."

This is a tragedy, Hughes concludes. By failing to experience deep friendships we rob ourselves along with our wives, children and others, because it's through relationships that we develop our full potential as men.

So how does one move from acquaintances to relationships? A good place to start might be to become what others are looking for in a real friend. And what's that? Proverbs 17:17 reports that the DNA of a genuine friend is that he "loves at all times." Whatever the obstacles to caring for the other person – our inconvenience, their screw-ups, etc.–a true friend, we're told, never fails to love. Is that possible?

It's not if we buy into our modern world's understanding of love. We're told that love is a feeling and therefore out of our control. People say, "I fell in love," like love is a ditch that we unwittingly stumble into and can't get out of. But if love is no more than a feeling, then loving "at all times" is impossible because, frankly, we don't always have loving feelings toward others. Is there more to love than feelings?

To find out I turned to the encyclopedia. Under "love" it said, "See 'emotion.'" Under "emotion" I found one lengthy article that used the word "love" twice and never defined it. No help there.

Next, being a red blooded American male, I looked up "sex." There I found a three-page article on the history of marriage. It mentioned "love" once. Still no definition. I thought, "It seems that in America we know a lot more about marriage and sex than we do about love." (Duh!) No help in the encyclopedia.

So I turned to the Bible. There I discovered some really interesting stuff on "love." For instance, in talking about love the Bible cites words like patience, kindness, protect, trust. Obviously, the Bible's view is that love isn't just something we say, it's something we do; a demonstration, not simply an inclination.

I also found that, rather than a feeling, the Bible defines love as a matter of the will. It would be pointless to command that we love one another, as the Bible does, if love is just a feeling. Feelings don't respond to commands, but the will does, or at least it can. Sure, love creates emotions, but love is not an emotion. It's a choice. Let's be honest, we don't fall out of love. We decide to stop loving. Hence the proverb exhorts us to love continually, that is, to determine always to act toward others in a caring way, no matter what.

The question remains, however, how is this possible? If the DNA of a genuine friend is to always do the loving thing, including when the loving thing is the last thing we feel like doing, how do we make our will override our feelings? A lot of times we can't, but God can. Only Jesus is always kind, always patient, always forgiving. Fortunately, he's willing to love others this way through us. We have only to ask him.

*From Hughes' book, "The Disciplines of a Godly Man"

...receiving a new heart

Essay 30: Building a "Great Society"

"By wisdom a house is built, and through understanding it is established; by knowledge its rooms are filled with all kinds of precious and pleasing treasures"–Proverbs 24:3-4

What are the essentials needed to build a prosperous and long-lasting nation? No idle question in these difficult times. What should we as a nation be doing in order to hand off to future generations a truly "Great Society"?

Proverbs 24:3-4 from the Bible draws on home building and decorating to depict symbolically how to construct a prosperous and long-lasting family, business enterprise or society. A man builds a house, and then fills it with beautiful furniture, paintings and tapestries. It's a pleasure to see such an elegant home.

The prevailing view today, of course, is that the building blocks for erecting an "elegant" America are education, legislation and environment. Maintaining a national focus on improving literacy, creating more laws to insure safety, and providing wholesome surroundings for all will, we're assured, one day issue in a kind of utopia.

So how's this strategy working out? I mean, America has invested trillions in these things. Where's the utopia we've been promised? Could it be that we've been following the wrong blueprint?

Clearly, education is crucial to our society's wellbeing. If we only give a starving man a fish, soon we create a man dependent on others for his food, and we rob him of his self-respect. On the other hand, if we teach the guy the basics of fishing, we give him dignity and the means to feed himself and even help others.

Legislation, too, is critical. Laws are essential for our protection from the criminal element and to deter crime. And few would deny that a healthy environment improves a young person's chances of becoming a well-rounded, productive adult.

But as important as education, legislation and environment are, I would argue that by themselves they'll never solve all our problems. Take education. Prior to WWII it was generally accepted that the world's finest universities were in Germany. In other words, these renowned institutions helped shape the culture that gave rise to one of the greatest evils ever known. So much for education as an elixir for the world's problems.

Nor is legislation an end all. True, the law provides a standard by which the egregiously unruly may be removed from society, but it does not produce good people. It does, however, expose the tendency in all of us to be lawbreakers. Who, for instance, would have thought to walk on the grass if there had been no sign forbidding it?

Environment doesn't hold the answer to the world's problems, either. HUD's failure to reverse longstanding life-style patterns should disabuse us of that notion. By the way, isn't it ironic that the decision that started everything spiraling downhill in the first place occurred in a perfect environment, the Garden of Eden?(!)

So what, if anything, will turn our nation around? Notice in the proverb that it's "by wisdom" that a house or a society is built. "Wisdom" here refers to the ancient scriptures of the Bible. The picture the Bible paints of man is that his most basic problem is not ignorance, lack of laws or a lousy environment, but the condition of his heart, which in turn limits the positive impact of education and these other things. As Alexander Solzhenitsyn wrote, "The line separating good and evil passes right through every human heart."

Put simply, solving America's problems, from the Bible's viewpoint, is fundamentally not about something happening outside of us – we get educated, pass laws, change our environment – but about something happening inside us. It says we need what only Jesus can provide, a new heart: "If anyone is in Christ, he is a new creation; the old has gone, the new has come." A "Great Society" starts there, one soul at a time.

...submitting to transcendent realities

Essay 31: Yielding to Life's Bigger Things

"Pride lands you flat on your face; humility prepares you for honors" – Proverbs 29:23

*There's an old story about a Navy warship that's navigating through dense fog one night when directly in their heading a distant, faint light appears. As they continue, the light grows brighter. At length the captain appears on the helm to assess the situation. About that time a voice over the radio calls on the vessel to adjust its course. The captain, an admiral, refuses to yield. Getting on the radio he demands, "No, you adjust your course."

Several transmissions follow between the admiral and what turns out to be an ensign, each calling on the other to yield. Finally, the admiral says, "We are a U. S. Navy carrier, you adjust." To which the ensign responds, "We're a lighthouse."

Some things are just bigger than we are; they transcend us. Take gravity, for example. Like the lighthouse, gravity invites us to adjust our course to its reality. If we do, we do well. But if we fail to yield to gravity's reality, no matter how strong we might be, we're going down.

Yielding to transcendent reality appears to be a simple matter of common sense, right? It would be except for the answer to a question that maybe more than anything else controls how we function in life. Here's the question: "Am I God, or not?"

While we of course recognize that we're not God, frankly sometimes we act like we are. Human beings have this tendency to overestimate our talents and importance and to think that life is all about us. Then, when we come up against a "lighthouse," operating under the delusion that we're "bigger," we founder on its realities.

It was this very thing that led to huge corporate meltdowns in recent years. Universal values such as justice, honesty, fidelity and responsibility comprise a category of bigger things that transcends us. You'll remember that a few senior executives chose to ignore these "lighthouses" and make their own self-centered interests the bigger thing. It all became a means to serve them. Theirs was the egocentric behavior that says, "I am God, and everything revolves around what I want," as opposed to, "I exist to serve the things that are bigger than I am." The result was predictable, these people not only foundered themselves, they took a lot of others down with them. Lighthouses always have the last say.

As with the admiral in the story above, we may at times be ignorant of life's bigger things. For instance, if we've reached the end of ourselves – life seems empty, meaning-less–we may not recognize that what we're missing is tran-scendence. That was my experience. Then I stumbled onto a transcendence that filled my emptiness. It was a person; his name is Jesus. "Come to me, and you'll recover your life," he promises. "Keep company with me, and you'll learn to live freely and lightly." And I've discovered him to be a man of his word. I might add that if he is in fact the transcendent reality the ancient scriptures claim him to be, then, like the lighthouse, we do well or suffer shipwreck depending on how we adjust to his reality.

A final thought. Henry Cloud writes in his book, "Integrity," that it is the bigger things, not ourselves, that make us big: "As we join them, we become larger." The paradox, Cloud continues, is that to join things bigger than we are, we have to humble ourselves by becoming smaller. "When we realize that we are smaller than the transcendent things, and we exist for *them* and not them for *us*, we grow into greatness." Proverbs 29:23 puts it this way, "...humility prepares you for honors."

*Many of the ideas in this article are drawn from Henry Cloud's book, "Integrity."

...practicing fanatical discipline

Essay 32: What Is Your "20-Mile March"?

"She brings him good, not harm, all the days of her life.... [A]nd shall be greatly praised" – Proverbs 31:12, 30

*Proverbs 31 is a verbal portrait a mother paints for her son, the king, to help him in his choice of a wife. The woman described in this passage embodies the core behavior of fanatical discipline. Every day, day after day, motivated by her love for God and with his help, she is industrious, frugal, efficient and productive. As a result she achieves a truly great enterprise: the perfect wife who brings her husband good all the days of her life and is therefore is highly honored.

The article following outlines how through their research Jim Collins and Morten Hansen discovered that the same core behavior endorsed in the Proverbs 31 wife is shared by companies and leaders that thrive even in tumultuous times.

To illustrate this trait, in their book, "Great by Choice," co-authors Collins and Hansen draw on the account of two teams of explorers who in October 1911 set out independently from the Antarctic coast determined to be the first humans to reach the South Pole. The team led by Norwegian Roald Amundsen got there 34 days ahead of Robert Scott's team. The Amundsen led team then returned to their base camp on the precise day they had planned. Scott and his team died on the way back.

"Good by Choice" answers the question: Why do some companies do well in uncertainty, even chaos, and others don't. The authors studied seven high-performing cases that they labeled "10X" companies because each beat its industry index by a factor of at least 10.

In their race to the Pole, Amundsen and Scott faced the same challenges of impossible weather, terrain, etc. Yet only Amundsen led his team to victory and safety. Collins' and Hansen's research indicated that a key core behavior separating these two men also separated the 10X business leaders from their less successful colleagues. You guessed it, fanatical discipline.

So how do we maintain a sense of control in a world that feels increasingly disoriented? "You do what Amundsen led his team to do," Collins advises: "You 'march 20 miles.'"

Amundsen's strategy for reaching the Pole and returning alive was to march 15 to 20 miles every day. Regardless of whether the conditions were favorable or unfavorable, Amundsen's expedition marched 20 miles. Scott followed a more irregular pattern. On a good day his team might travel 40 miles. If they faced a blizzard, they waited it out in their tents.

Amundsen's philosophy required fanatical discipline, pushing ahead in the worst conditions, and, when the sun was shining, exercising self-control by not going too far. Such was Amundsen's resolve that with the team only 45 miles from the Pole, and things working well, and their reaching the Pole first at risk because they didn't know where Scott was, instead of pressing on, after 17 miles they rested that day. Why? If they got to the Pole exhausted and a storm hit, they might not survive.

Collins found that 10X companies practiced similar radical restraint. Southwest Airlines, for example, in a notoriously brutal industry demanded of itself a profit every year (their "20-mile march"). In January 2014 the company reported its 41st year of consecutive profitability.

Equally important, in boom times, when their less-successful peers were rapidly expanding, Southwest had the discipline not to risk overstretching their resources and putting their "20-mile march" in jeopardy. In 1996, Southwest opened four cities to their service although more than 100 cities clamored for it.

So as we begin 2015, maybe a good question to ask ourselves would be, "Going forward, what will be my 20-mile march?"

What are actions that if practiced with the fanatical discipline of consistent, consecutive performance (perhaps calling on God for help, as the Proverbs 31 wife) would make our lives more a truly great enterprise?

*In addition to an October 2011"Fortune" article by Jim Collins titled "Great by Choice," in writing this essay I used a presentation of the same title that Collins delivered at the 2012 Willow Creek Association Global Leadership Summit.

...countering the snares of selfishness

Essay 33: It's All about Me. Or Is It?

"Selfishness only causes trouble..."–Proverbs 28:25

Googling "self" turned up all sorts of categories: self-directed, self-reliance, self-centered, self-serving, and self-important, to name a few. There's even a "Self Magazine." It turns out we're a deeply "self"-conscious society. I'm shocked! Aren't you? Not!

You may recall Abraham Maslow's hierarchy of needs. It's still a very popular framework in sociology research, management training and secondary and higher psychology instruction. What's the pinnacle of Maslow's hierarchy, i.e., mankind's greatest ambition? Would you believe self-actualization? You bet.

Baby Boomers have long been libeled, er, labeled, the "me" generation. But this "It's all about me" stuff didn't start with us. In 1940, for example, C.S. Lewis wrote in "The Problem of Pain," "At this very moment you and I are either committing [selfishness], or about to commit it, or repenting it."

Unfortunately, this problem may actually be getting worse. In today's Wall Street Journal, Peter Kann writes concerning NBC anchor Brian Williams' undoing, "In part Mr. Williams is symptomatic of larger social trends where traditional virtues like modesty and privacy have given way to the spotlight of self-promotion, here even lives too pedestrian for the paparazzi become an endless series of selfies."

In light of our natural preoccupation with self, it's a bummer that selfishness equates with trouble, as the Brian Williams' story and Proverbs 28:25 remind us. Other examples of this "trouble" include of course how hard self-centeredness is on marriages. After interviewing hundreds of folks searching for self-fulfillment, psychology professor Daniel Yankelovich concluded, "Among married people that I interviewed, those most devoted to their own self-fulfillment were those having the most trouble in their marriage." No kidding!

And then there's frustration and despair resulting from me-ism. Witness Sherman McCoy, hero of Tom Wolfe's novel "The Bonfire of the Vanities." Believing himself to be the master of his own universe, McCoy's life unravels when a freak car accident reveals that he doesn't have control of everything after all. Imagine that!

Thus far, this essay has not been too encouraging. It gets better. There's hope. While Proverbs warns of the consequences of selfishness, scripture elsewhere offers ways to counter man's albatross. For instance, building strong relationships. The Bible confirms in 1 Corinthians that we're social creatures: "In God's plan men and women need each other." We share an essential need to be interested in other people, and building into a relationship tends to take the spotlight off of "me."

Another self-centeredness antidote is giving ourselves away through service. Ephesians explains that "God planned that we should spend our lives helping others." Coaching little league, mentoring a colleague, making hospital visits, being a servant leader in the marketplace – whenever we give ourselves with no expectation of a payback, it offsets self-centeredness.

A third and maybe the most powerful counter to selfishness is what the Bible calls "self-denial." Jesus says in Luke's Gospel, "If you want to come with me, you must forget yourself, take up your cross every day, and follow me." This is where we get involved in stuff – the messy, tragic lives of others, for example – that no one else wants to do. Jesus exemplified this by washing a dozen fisherman's filthy feet and pouring out his life sacrificially for you and me.

"Man is born to trouble as sure as sparks fly upward" (Job). The culprit? Selfishness, mankind's fundamental defect. It first reared its ugly head in Eden ("We can be like God"), resulting in the curse; it continues creating havoc today in your life and mine. Part of our DNA, we can't root it out entirely, but with God helping us to focus on building relationships, serving and sacrificing, we can mitigate its troublesome effects. Or putting a more positive twist on it, to give all, instead of scheming to get all, according to Jesus, is to know what it means to "really" live.

...dodging causes of failure

Essay 34: Avoiding Life's Pitfalls

"Hey, I'm only human." Ever heard that excuse? Sure. Everybody has failures. Screw-ups are part of the human condition. On the other hand, there's no reason for us to make all the mistakes in life. So, since forewarned is forearmed, it might be helpful to consider a few proverbs that warn of sure causes of failure in order that we may take steps to avoid these pitfalls.

One sure way to fail, according to Proverbs, is to inadequately plan: "A sensible man watches for problems ahead and prepares to meet them. The simpleton never looks and suffers the consequences" (27:12).

"Never looking" played a dominant role, for example, in Hitler's decision to order his 6th Army, encircled at Stalingrad, to fight on, rather than break out and retreat. "Der Fuhrer" listened to his air marshal's assurances that the Luftwaffe could supply the army with an "air bridge." What the careless air marshal failed to take into account was that while the Luftwaffe's maximum daily lift capacity was 300 tons, the 6th Army needed 500 tons of supplies each day. This planning failure contributed significantly to the disaster that befell the 6th Army: Only 6,000 of a quarter of a million soldiers returned to Germany. He who fails to plan plans to fail.

A second pitfall leading to failure that Proverbs warns against is pride. When we start believing, "Well, you know, I really am too good, too smart, too experienced, too whatever to fail," a downfall is not far away: "Pride leads to destruction and arrogance to downfall" (16:18).

One symptom of pride is thinking we don't need anybody's advice. The tragedy is that we're surrounded by friends, colleagues and counselors who because of hard-earned, examined experience have a wealth of wisdom to offer on business decisions, money issues, relationship quandaries, etc. But too often because of pride we say, "I don't need any help." So in our arrogance we set out to reinvent the wheel, vastly increasing the odds of failure.

Third, Proverbs tells us that failure comes when we avoid taking risks: "Fear of man is a dangerous trap" (29:25). Allowing concerns for our image to drive our decisions – "What will others think if I fail? – positions us to lose. During the Civil War, General McClellan, fearful of risk, fumbled the opportunity to end the war three years and half a million lives early. On the Confederate side, General Ewell, equally risk averse, squandered a chance to seize the high ground at Gettysburg, arguably the cause of Lee's defeat in the battle that was the turning point of the war. Fear of trying assures failure.

So does giving up too soon: "A lazy fellow has trouble all through life" (15:19). We fail when we are too lazy to work at it and just quit. Somebody pointed out that the value of a postage stamp is its ability to stick to one thing until it gets there. It's also true that an oak tree is just a little nut that refused to give its ground. Sometimes we fail simply because we give ground too soon.

But perhaps the most common cause of failure is turning a deaf ear to our Creator. Proverbs notes that, "There is a way that seems right to a man, but in the end it leads to death" (14:12). Getting, chasing greatness, seeking to be honored–these things seem so obviously the path to success, but, ironically, they instead lead to failure. Who would guess that success in life comes through things like giving, sacrificing and serving others? But then, according to the scriptures, God does say, "My ways are not your ways." It turns out that intuition is a poor substitute for the Bible's guidelines for living.

...engaging in personal growth

Essay 35: A Matter of Life and Death

"My child, listen to what I say, and treasure my commands.... Then you will...find the right way to go. For wisdom and truth will enter the very center of your being..." – Proverbs 2:1, 9-10

*We know that if something is alive, it's doing two things simultaneously, growing and dying. Usually one of these processes is more dominant, or at least more visible. When our young children were developing their motor skills that would serve them well in life, the last thing we noticed was that they were also getting older and moving toward death.

We also know that the relationship between growing and dying is greatly affected by use. Think of this in terms of our muscles. The more we use them, the more they grow and increase in capacity, reversing the death process, or at least slowing it down. The same with out brains. At one time scientists thought that the number of brain cells we had at birth was all we were going to get. We now understand that the brain can grow and with use can develop even in old age. Literally, use creates life. Studies suggest that mentally challenging lives that focus on growth delay or prevent dementia.

Unfortunately, our desire to grow into more than we are can be stifled. When we no longer have an appetite for personal growth, we can drift into a state of "maintain," where we just continue to be the way we are, day after day. We can relate to our spouses, kids, friends and coworkers the same way, never wanting to grow into relating more deeply. We can dull ourselves with TV, romance novels, video games, etc.

Since personal growth, then, is no less than a matter of life and death, it's essential for us to understand what's required to create growth.

The law of entropy says that "closed" systems, systems without a connection to things outside themselves, naturally die. But "open" systems can grow into a higher state of being, provided they have access to an external energy source. Translated into people, this means that to grow, we must be "open." If we think we know everything worth knowing already, we will be closed to new experiences and sources of development. Rather than growth, the result will be disintegration.

When someone is open, there's the possibility for an energy infusion. They may look to connect to an outside energy source to push them to grow–a counselor, a group, or a community of growth. They may go to seminars and retreats, where they study, refresh, get input into their soul and re-create. They may establish an accountability relationship, get an advanced degree, or submit themselves to a mentor.

So, there are two options on the table: be open to connecting to outside energy sources that stimulate growth, or be closed to new input and begin to atrophy. A no-brainer choice, right? Maybe. Oh, I know what the "right" choice is, the one I should make, but opting to maintain, particularly as I grow older, can be awfully attractive. That's why it seems to me that the choice we make here (and may well need to make repeatedly), in Proverbs 2 parlance, goes to "the very center of our being," to the level of our character, who we are and what motivates us down deep.

I find that this is where the Bible can help. Frankly, sometimes my character needs a boost in order that I might keep on being open, keep on looking to make the most of my life. The Proverbs 2 passage above tells me that God wants to help me with this. He who has all wisdom knows the right way to go and, as long as I stay connected to him, motivates me to keep going that way.

*With help from Henry Cloud's book, "Integrity"

...answering the highest call

Essay 36: Saying No to "Caesar"

"When the righteous triumph, there is great elation; but when the wicked rise to power, men go into hiding" – Proverbs 28:12

At the close of WWII the Allies brought war crimes charges against former Nazi leaders. Many of the accused maintained in their defense that since they were simply following lawful orders, it would be unjust to convict them. What the Nuremburg judges had to decide was, is it ever not only right, but necessary to disobey authority.

The dictionary defines "authority" as "one who has power to influence or command thought, opinion or behavior." Authority is of course integral to government; the military; the business, academic and ecclesiastical worlds; and the family. In all of these areas power is exercised with the expectation of obedience. Are there exceptions to this expectation? Is disobedience to authority ever justified, even necessary? If so, on what grounds?

The New Testament book of Romans, in chapter 13, outlines the ancient scriptures' perspective on authority: "Everyone must submit himself to the governing authorities, for there is no authority except that which God has established.... Consequently, he who rebels against the authority is rebelling against what God has instituted, and those who do so will bring judgment on themselves.... For he is God's servant to do you good."

These verses assert that authority was God's idea, and that he established it for our good. We may not always look at authority as a good thing, but consider how chaotic and dangerous life would be without the police, the military, etc. Roman 13 also declares that because all human authorities derive their "right to rule" from God, i.e., act as God's agents, to rebel against our authorities is to defy God and invite consequences.

This passage of course assumes that our authority does not require something contrary to God's moral law, as revealed in the scriptures. But what about when those in power create laws that are clearly in opposition to the laws of the Creator? Surely this would constitute an exception to the obedience that Romans 13 requires.

And so it does. In the Gospel of Matthew we're told that a group of religious professionals approached Jesus hoping to trick him into either making a treasonous statement or alienating his supporters. "Tell us," they said, "is it right to pay taxes to Caesar or not?" Sensing their treachery, Jesus held up a Roman coin and asked, "Whose portrait is this? And whose inscription?" They said, "Caesar's." "Then," said Jesus, "give to Caesar what is Caesar's, and to God what is God's."

The principle here is that "Caesar" is to be obeyed within the bounds of his authority. If, however, to obey him would violate God's moral law – as in Nazi Germany, for instance – then Caesar has exceeded his authority, and we must say no to Caesar.

In closing, here are a couple examples that fall closer to home. Much has been made lately of whether the government may fine owners of closely-held businesses who, because of their sincerely held religious beliefs, refuse to provide their employees with health insurance that includes abortion services. In addition, some states have passed laws requiring business owners to deliver services that violate their scripture-informed consciences. I would suggest to you that these are cases of "Caesar" exceeding his rightful authority (the Founders understood this, which is why the First Amendment to the Constitution forbids the making of any law that impedes the free exercise of religion). In such instances Christ-followers not only may, but, if they are to obey God, must decline to obey Caesar...and be prepared to accept the consequences.

...seeking advice from the wise

Essay 37: Putting the Pedal to the Metal of Our Dreams

"Plans fail for lack of counsel, but with many advisers they succeed" – Proverbs 15:22

*Imagine trying to get somewhere in a car without using the accelerator. A trip at idle speed would be more like travailing than traveling, but with the pedal to the metal so to speak we reach our destination in a reasonable amount of time.

Solomon, "the wisest of men," speaks in the Bible book of Proverbs of another kind of "accelerator." With this accelerator disengaged, Solomon advises that achieving great dreams is virtually impossible. It doesn't take much idling along, making minimal progress, for most people to bail out on their dreams. But Solomon's accelerator changes this narrative. Engaged properly, it moves us at top speed to the achievement of our dreams. What is this accelerator, this putting the pedal to the metal of our dreams? According to Proverbs 15:22, it's seeking advice, getting counsel.

Unfortunately, it's human nature to look for a counselor only "after" we run into trouble. We men are especially guilty of this. Only as a last resort do we ask for directions. (Our salvation is GPS. Unless of course it fails.) Solomon asserts that obtaining counsel "before" stuff goes south is critical to success.

A couple examples: According to the financial data company Bloomberg L.P., eight out of 10 entrepreneurs who start a business fail within the first 18 months. The stats on matrimony aren't much better; 50% of married couples end up in divorce court. Amazingly, these failure rates are cut by two-thirds when counselors become part of the equation "before" the business is started or the marriage vows exchanged.

We've all said things like, "I did the best I could." "I can't do it any better." "This is as good as it gets." Such statements may be true in the sense that they reflect the limits of our capabilities when we're trying to do something on our own, but they're often false in the sense that with counsel we could have done much more.

In the early 70s I had a plan that I was convinced would yield an excellent return on my money. While in Vietnam, I had put all my pay into the government's savings program. This netted me about $5,000 ($27,000 in today's money), which I invested at 12% interest in a private college about which I knew almost nothing. Naturally, I sought no one's counsel. A year later, I lost the $5,000 plus interest when the college closed its doors after its president ran off with the school's money along with his secretary. Failed plans, notes Solomon in Proverbs 15:22, are the fruit of lack of counsel.

Success, on the other hand, Solomon reminds us, comes with many advisors. For several years I participated on a four-man leadership team that represented a group with two different philosophies on how our organization should function. Fortunately, both points of view were reflected on the leadership team. This made reaching consensus more difficult, but had all four of us embraced the same philosophy leaving no one to advocate for the other perspective, there's little doubt that we would have alienated half the people, guaranteeing the failure of the organization. With many advisors, however, we achieved success.

It's important we recognize that Solomon's accelerator comes with a warning label. In Proverbs 25:19 he compares biting down on an abscessed tooth to the pain stemming from relying on an unfaithful counselor. In other words, it's dumb to take advice from just anybody. In other proverbs

Solomon strongly recommends that we look for qualities such as wisdom (14:7) and integrity (10:20) in our advisors.

To conclude, if the Bible is true, then God alone is perfect in wisdom and integrity, and he alone knows precisely what works in our world and what doesn't. This would of course make him the perfect counselor. Even better, scripture says that God gives his flawless guidance to all who in faith ask him for it. Something to think about.

*Adapted from Steven Scott's "The Richest Man Who Ever Lived"

Category 3

Then you will know the truth, and the truth will set you free. – Jesus Christ
(The Gospel of John 8:32)

Essays 38-52:

According to Proverbs, scriptural truth...

...is superior to conventional wisdom

Essay 38: Two Kinds of Wisdom

Conventional wisdom, according to Wikipedia, is "The body of ideas or explanations generally accepted as true by the public or by experts in a field." Wikipedia goes on to say that "Such ideas or explanations, though widely held, are unexamined." They're not necessarily true, in other words.

Take for instance conventional wisdom's contention that money plus possessions equals satisfaction. Now I know we say we don't believe that, but sometimes we act as if we do, though even a cursory study of the lives of the world's wealthiest people quickly belies this notion. Then there's what surveys tell us about the majority of high school and college students today accepting as true the belief that it's alright to cheat to get ahead. The ruinous consequences of this worldview are evident in the lives of countless dishonored and failed politicians, CEOs, entrepreneurs, and religious leaders who carried this attitude into their professional lives. Conventional wisdom also holds that education is the answer to society's ills. Yet the German people were arguably the best educated in the world when Adolph Hitler and his Nazi party rose to power.

Conventional wisdom is at best a shaky foundation on which to build a life. Such "wisdom" may, of course, eventually give rise to a successful life. I mean, after we try out some of these phony ideas and run up against their fallacies, we can learn from our failures and try to avoid making the same mistake twice. But I'd suggest that there's a better way to obtain wisdom than just learning through the school of hard knocks. Allow me to explain.

In the Bible, depending on the context, two different English words translate the Old Testament term "hokma." Hokma, in English translations, is rendered "skill" in several verses to describe the ability of some individuals to take raw materials and transform them into beautiful furniture, jewelry, etc. In other verses hokma is translated "wisdom" to refer to ideas and principles that when acted on with discipline and God's help transform a "raw" life into a thing of beauty. So while conventional wisdom, because it's not always true, is a poor foundation on which to try to build a life of excellence, hokma is exactly what's needed because it's always true, or so the Bible claims.

Here's an example of conventional wisdom versus the Bible's hokma ("wisdom"). Conventional wisdom says that it doesn't matter if we look at porn, listen to gangsta rap and play blood and guts video games because, "Well, you know, I'm not affected by any of that stuff." Hokma, on the other hand, warns us to ruthlessly guard our heart, what we allow to enter our mind, because our thoughts shape how we live our life. So on which of these two perspectives do you think the Madison Avenue people base their multi-billion-dollar advertising budgets?

Another example. Conventional wisdom holds that conflict is always, if possible, to be avoided. If one must engage in it, the end goal is "I win, you lose." But Hokma recognizes that there are times when conflict is desirable because it surfaces issues in need of resolution. Take in a marriage, for instance. Conflict between a husband and wife can serve as a venue for open and honest discussion, which can lead to greater understanding between the two and, in turn, a better relationship. In such cases hokma teaches that, through humility, gentleness and patience, unity can be restored, and both sides can win. Now which of these approaches would you say is characteristic of a life of excellence?

Proverbs 13:14, referring to the hokma variety of wisdom, declares that "The teaching of the wise is a fountain of life, turning a man from the snares of death." Makes sense, doesn't it?

...is the basis for character development

Essay 39: Can the "Leopard" Change His Spots?

Recently, Maj Gen (Ret) Nick Krawciw gave a talk on leadership to a group I'm associated with. Gen Krawciw has impeccable leadership credentials. During his 31 years of service in the U.S. Army he commanded at all levels, from platoon to division. In 2006, in recognition of his "inspirational leadership," West Point presented Gen Krawciw the 2006 Distinguished Graduate Award.

In speaking to our group Nick explained, "Rather than searching for a perfect definition of leadership I prefer to think of the attributes that are essential in good leadership." Topping that list, he noted, is character, which "involves integrity, honor, courage, loyalty, creativity and other similar fundamental values that lead to trust."

Those instilling core values of solid character into Nick's life include his dad and mom, who in addition to showing him "the importance of faith in God," modeled "love, encouragement, and self-sacrificing care" throughout the very difficult years of World War II in Europe (where Nick was born and spent his early youth).

Two years after immigrating to the U.S., Nick enrolled at Bordentown Military Institute, where the motto was "rather be than seem." There, the headmaster not only trusted Nick to pay off his tuition debt years later, without interest, but also through daily chapel talks became "an important senior mentor for me."

As a cadet at West Point, Nick was required to participate in weekly discussions about the meaning of honor and integrity. On active duty he was involved in continuous character development: As a commander, there were "many opportunities" to set the example, make mistakes, accept responsibility, and make it right. In higher-level assignments he was able to learn from the examples of men like Lt Gen (Ret) Walter Ulmer, "a person with integrity and moral courage."

Gen Krawciw's comments raise a question. What about those who, unlike the General, didn't have a lot of positive role models, especially when growing up? Or maybe we did, but we managed to ignore them. Psychologists tell us that the character traits that will define an individual can be clearly identified as early as age seven. Can adults change behaviors that have been deeply etched into their psyche?

The Bible says that absolutely we can. St Peter is a famous example. He goes from faint-heartedly denying his Lord, not once but three times, to becoming the leader of the early church movement whose character is a source of inspiration, challenge and encouragement to many. At the end of his life he suffers death rather than deny his Lord again.

How does "the leopard" change his spots? Here's the answer from Proverbs 2:1-9: To those who "apply their heart to understanding and cry out for insight...the Lord gives wisdom" to consistently make choices that are "right and just and fair."

The implication of these verses is that mentors and on the job character training, desirable as these things are, are not the only way or even necessarily the best way to build character. Proverbs asserts that the most direct route to developing courage, loyalty, integrity, etc. is to acquire wisdom through a diligent search of the scriptures. Then, through depending on God to apply his wisdom to our lives, strong character will emerge, enabling us to consistently make choices that are right and just and fair. It's never too late for a character upgrade.

...is about what's "right," not what "works"

Essay 40: Pragmatism Trumps Principle

*Should we be concerned to do what's "right" or be satisfied with doing what works? Some would argue that if something works, that makes it right, a philosophy called pragmatism.

Pragmatism was a late-nineteenth-century brainchild of John Dewey–the father of modern education–and several others. Theological skeptics, these men popularized the notion that since there is no absolute truth, good can be measured in terms of what works. In other words, if it works, do it.

But what is the measure of what "works"? Enter utilitarianism, the philosophy holding that something works when it results in the greatest good for the greatest number.

What could possibly be wrong with the idea that doing the greatest good for the greatest number is always the right thing to do? Well, history is full of examples of unchecked pragmatism leading to tyranny. How often have governments seized on the excuse that they were acting in the interest of the majority to persecute some minority group?

In contrast to pragmatism the Bible claims that what's "right" is not determined by someone's arbitrary opinion of what will do the greatest good for the greatest number, but by timeless moral principles established by a good and just God. For instance, "Where there is no word from God, people are uncontrolled, but those who obey what they have been taught are happy" (Proverbs 29:18). He says that it's when people are governed by God's moral principles, not by pragmatism or some man-made standard, that society as a whole, including the vulnerable, truly benefits.

So what about twenty-first-century America, do we lean toward pragmatism or principle? Here's a clue: In 2002, the Barna Research group did a national survey. People were asked if they believe that there are unchanging moral absolutes or that moral truth is relative to the circumstances. By a 3 to 1 margin they said truth is always relative to the situation – if it works, do it. People held that pragmatism trumps principle.

Here's another clue: In one of the earlier budget crises, when Republican Senator Lindsay Graham was criticized for saying that the banks might have to be nationalized, he responded, "It's not responsible to take options off the table that might work." Another example of pragmatism over principle.

On the other side, President Obama appointed William Lynn, a lobbyist for a defense contractor, as deputy secretary of defense, even though the President had given notice that no lobbyist would be asked to join his administration to work on matters he or she had lobbied on during the previous two years. Why the waiver? Obama said Lynn knew how to make things work. Again, pragmatism over principle.

Of course it's always easy to wag a finger. The truth is we have all at times slipped into pragmatism, doing whatever is necessary to get the job done versus what's right, especially when under pressure. In these days of uncertainty, it would probably be a good idea to pray for our political leaders. We might also do well to remember that choosing "right" over what "works" puts us in step with the One the Bible claims is all-wise and therefore in a better position than anyone to know what really is the greatest good for the greatest number.

*Adapted from article of the same title by Chuck Colson

...offers ethics that drive significance

Essay 41: Where Do Your Values Come From?

"A life devoted to things is a dead life, a stump; a God-shaped life is a flourishing tree" – Proverbs 11:28

Values drive behavior. What we decide is most important in life will control and direct us. Jesus said it best: "Where your treasure is, that's where your heart's going to be." It follows then that nothing is more important to a leader's effectiveness than values, and that makes where we find our values critical.

Surveys indicate that as many as 80% of Americans believe that our society's values are in transition, that in fact our culture is suffering a morals meltdown. Ya think maybe this perception has anything to do with the fact that for years now there's been an explosive growth of Hollywood's endorsement of infidelity and divorce as the norm, of internet smut, of "the ends justify the means" politics, of an entitlement mentality, of "just make sure it doesn't make the papers" business ethics, etc.?

What's triggered this crisis of moral decline? I'd like to suggest that the genesis of the problem can be summed up in two words: truth decay. Mainstream America today values feelings over truth. For example, you may remember that in 2006, when James Frey's book "A Million Little Pieces" was exposed as a literary fraud, there was a public outcry from Oprah and others defending Frey as an "emotional truth-teller," whatever that means. Many in our society today would say, "If something makes me feel good, I don't care whether it's true or not."

This is a major shift in thinking in America over the last seventy years. The generation that fought World War II generally agreed on what was true–what was right and what was wrong. But today, nothing stirs up trouble like somebody saying, "This is true, and that's wrong." What happened?

Relativism happened. Relativism says what's truth for you isn't necessarily truth for me. Though defying logic, this philosophy has our culture by the jugular, as the dominance today of relativism's supreme value, tolerance, clearly demonstrates. Our society values tolerance over truth, which is why we don't want to say the truth. We might offend somebody, thereby committing the worst of all possible sins.

Due largely to relativism, what once was called right in America is now called wrong, and vice versa. Remember when as school kids we were challenged by the apocryphal story of George Washington and the cherry tree to always tell the truth? Studies today reveal that up to 95% of high-school students feel that the pressure to get ahead justifies cheating. Nowadays, pornographers are nominated for academy awards while a first-grade boy who kisses a little girl is accused of sexual harassment. Go figure! Hence the question, how can I live a life of value in a world that can't decide what's right and what's wrong?

What values "should" drive my behavior? Values derive from only three possible sources: One, I can get my values from an internal source. That's where I say, "My values are based on me, because I know so much. I will decide if something is right or wrong according to how it feels."

Two, I can determine to get my values from an external source: "I'll listen to talk shows and watch the polls, and I'll ignore the fact that the culture's values, confused by self-interest, social conditioning and situational ethics, are shallow and subjective."

Three, I can turn to the eternal source: "I choose God's values because he's the creator and therefore the measure of truth."

According to Proverbs 11:28, while values derived from choice three inspire behaviors that lead to a life of significance - fruitfulness and vitality - those stemming from choices one and two drive behaviors that lead to deadness - fruitlessness and ruin. At one time or another I've drawn my values from all three of these possible sources. My experience, hands down, is that, just as the Bible asserts, choice-three values yield far better results.

...explains life's puzzles

Essay 42: The Reason for the Season

"The king's heart is like a stream of water directed by the Lord; he guides it wherever he pleases" - Proverbs 21:1
*In America today Christmas has become a Santa-ized, materialized blur. In many quarters what is seen as just another celebration is referred to in PC terms like "Happy Holidays" and "Seasons Greetings" by folks who can't bring themselves to use the word "Christmas." As a result, it's easy

to lose touch with the event that's the reason for the season. The goal of this article is to use the answer to a Christmas question to reconnect us with what the Bible claims is the reality of Christmas.

Here's the question: Why Bethlehem? In the Bible account Jesus was born in Bethlehem, a humble village a day's walk south of Jerusalem. Why there? Why not in Rome, capital of the ancient world, or in Jerusalem, spiritual center of Judaism? Why in the insignificant little town of Bethlehem?

Christmas dawned in Bethlehem because the accuracy of the ancient Hebrew scriptures required that he be born nowhere else. I'll explain.

In Genesis, God speaks to a man named Abraham. If Abraham will demonstrate his trust in God by abandoning his support network in what today is Iraq and following God's directions to an unnamed country, God promises to "bless all the peoples of the earth through him."

Abraham eventually complies. God then leads him and his wife to Palestine. As for God's promise to bless peoples everywhere through Abraham, the many examples include Joseph, Abraham's great-grandson, who became prime minister of Egypt and saved tens of thousands worldwide from starvation. Through Moses, another descendant, came the Ten Commandments, the foundation of Western jurisprudence.

But many passages in the Old Testament and, later, in the New Testament assert that the ultimate fulfillment of God's promise to Abraham will come through his descendant known as the Messiah, or the Christ. We're told that he will be God's provision for forgiveness and eternal life for people of all races. Why Bethlehem? Thousands of years before his birth the Bible predicted that the Christ would be born a son of Abraham.

But birth into just any Jewish family wouldn't do. Genesis notes that the Messiah will be of the Israelite tribe of Judah. And in 2 Samuel, King David, himself a son of Judah, is told that the Messiah will descend from him.

So what's the connection between David and a manger in Bethlehem? After the Israelites conquered Palestine, they divided the land among the 12 tribes. Judah's slice of the pie included Bethlehem, where David was born and spent his youth. To emphasize the relationship between David and his descendant, the Messiah, God arranged for Jesus to be born in the village known as "the city of David."

Why Bethlehem? Because it was foretold that the Messiah would be Jewish, of the tribe of Judah, from David's family. There's more. At Christmas we sing "Oh Little Town of Bethlehem" because the Old Testament prophet Micah specifically identifies Bethlehem as the birthplace of God's Son.

But the most intriguing aspect of this story has to be how Joseph and Mary came to be in Bethlehem at the time of Mary's delivery. You remember it says that Caesar Augustus decreed that everybody return to his hometown to get on the tax rolls. Like many powerful people today, Caesar thought he was calling the shots. The truth, as Proverb 21:1 explains, is that God is in control. He decided that Caesar would make this decree insuring that Joseph and Mary would be in Bethlehem – about 100 miles from their home in Nazareth–at the very moment Mary went into labor with her firstborn, a son, God's Son, the Messiah. The star would lead the Magi to Bethlehem, not Nazareth.

God moved men, nations, whole civilizations, even the heavens to bring to pass the birth of Jesus Christ. And for one reason: That we might have a Savior. Merry Christmas!

*Adapted from remarks by Rick Warren

...protects from a prodigal lifestyle

Essay 43: Equipped for Success

I think most of us would agree that the right equipment can spell the difference between success and failure. You wouldn't want your surgeon working on you with a chain saw or your dentist with woodworking drill. I've noticed that professionals are quite particular about their tools. Whether it's a surgeon, a dentist, a fisherman, or a mountain climber, professionals know that their success depends on using the right equipment.

I'd like to suggest for your consideration that it also takes using the right equipment if we are to experience the kind of successful, satisfying life we all long for.

Wouldn't it be great if life came with a set of instructions designed to keep us from colliding with reality in painful ways? Hey, talk about a piece of equipment that could make the difference between success and failure. Figuring life out can be like trying to work a giant jigsaw puzzle without a picture to follow, or, even worse, with the wrong picture to follow. But what if there was a kind of "owner's manual" for life that we could rely on to always give us the right picture?

"Not so fast," somebody says. "I don't need a set of instructions. I trust my own "seat of the pants" navigation, you know, just doing what seems like the right thing for me." Let's consider that for a moment.

Lee Iacocca may be the best-known U.S. automotive executive since Henry Ford. Navigating life by the seat of his pants, Iacocca, described as an aggressive, dictatorial leader, clawed his way to the top of the heap, first at Ford, then at Chrysler. He expected his success to provide satisfaction and significance. Sadly, when he reached the top of the corporate ladder, all he found there were pigeon droppings.

"Here I am," he wrote in his autobiography, "in the twilight years of my life still wondering what it's all about. I can tell you this, fame and fortune is for the birds." Few things in life, as someone said, are as tragic as being successful at the wrong thing.

Iacocca's story illustrates a phenomenon called "positive illusion," which is psych speak for our tendency to have a warped perspective when it comes to anything involving ourselves. Do you know why 25% of people believe they're in the top 1% in their ability to get along with others, and why the vast majority of us consider ourselves above-average? Positive illusion.

Positive illusion is what's wrong with "seat of the pants" navigation. Lee Iacocca is a smart guy. No doubt he was aware that most people's experience is that money doesn't buy them happiness. But because of positive illusion, he concluded that he would be the exception. It didn't work out that way.

In wrapping this up, I refer you back to the owner's manual idea. What if there were a storehouse of information, understood to apply to all, with maxims warning, for example, against "seat of the pants" navigation. Maxims such as, "What you think is the right road may lead to death." And, "Wisdom is worth more than silver; it brings more profit than gold"? If Lee Iacocca had taken heed of such a manual, it's likely he would have found what his heart longed for.

The above citations are maxims from – no surprise here–the Bible (Proverbs 14:12 and 3:14), which claims to be the owner's manual for life. But can we depend on the scriptures to reveal how life really works, to protect us from "positive illusion" and similar hazards that can lead to a wasted life? You might want to check them out for yourself.

...circumvents failings of other worldviews

Essay 44: John Lennon Was Right after All

"The king's heart is in the hand of the Lord; he directs it like a watercourse wherever he pleases" – Proverbs 21:1.

It turns out that Beatle John Lennon was right in a 1971 appearance on the Dick Cavett Show when he gave his take on the big scare of the day: overpopulation. "I think whatever happens will balance itself out...I don't really believe it," said Lennon. "It's alright for us all living to say, 'Well, there's enough of us [people] so we won't have any more'...I don't believe in that."

That was a major counter-cultural statement in 1971. Back then, all the experts warned that world population was a perilous threat to the future of mankind. And, as John Stonestreet noted in a BreakPoint article, "Bugs in the Overpopulation Theory," "No one shouted that alarm more loudly than Dr. Paul Ehrlich, the Stanford biologist behind the explosive bestseller, 'The Population Bomb.'"

Ehrlich forecast that hundreds of millions would starve due to the "utter breakdown in the capacity of the planet to support humanity." Half of Americans would die by the end of the '80s, he confidently warned, and by 2000, India and China would self-destruct. Ehrlich insisted on immediate incentives and penalties to limit population growth.

The result of his call to reduce child bearing? The U.S. birth rate is 1.9 today, down from 2.6 in the late '60s when the "The Population Bomb" was published. For sure, other factors bear on America's falling fertility rate – more women working, the expense and demands of parenthood, the pursuit of "happiness" as life's lodestar, etc.–but nothing has contributed more to this trend than Ehrlich's "terrifying jeremiad that humankind stood on the brink of apocalypse" (from "The Unrealized Horrors of Population Explosion," a piece by Clyde Haberman the New York Times ran this month).

What's wrong with a 1.9 fertility rate? It takes 2.1 to sustain population. Our numbers have continued to grow due to the 40+ million people in America born elsewhere. However, rapidly falling birth rates in many developing nations, including Mexico (7.3 in 1960 to 2.2 in 2013), translate to fewer immigrants. We are on course to begin shrinking soon. Likely results include endemic economic stagnation–where Japan (1.3 fertility rate) is today – too few workers to sustain social-security programs for retirees, and a weakened military defense because of lack of money and military-age manpower.

While America's impending population crisis reflects the thesis of Ehrlich's book, the truly draconian impact of his ideas are evident in other parts of the world where they took root. For example, throughout the '70s, India's government surgically sterilized more than eight million women, many forcibly, some lethally. China, with its infamous One Child Policy, took even more drastic measures.

As you may have noticed, hundreds of millions did not starve in the '70s. Although the planet's population has doubled since Ehrlich's book, fewer people today suffer from hunger than when he made his dire predictions. How come? The world figured out how to feed itself despite its rising numbers – a development that was outside of Ehrlich's worldview.

On a video attached to Haberman's Times article Indian Economist Gita Sen, explaining Ehrlich's failed forecast, told the Times, "There's a tendency to apply to human beings the same sort of models that may apply for the insect world. The difference of course is that human beings are conscious beings, and we do all kinds of things to change our destiny."

Stonestreet observes that what Sen refers to as "destiny" the Bible calls providence. Proverbs 21:1 explains that God controls the course of human events so as to bring about his purpose. Stonestreet: "Part of God's control is exhibited in the creativity and innovation humans are just so good at – and which can be used for evil, but can also be used for good. In short, [the Bible] sees human beings as [bearers of God's image], not insects."

...promotes self-confidence

Essay 45: To Be, or Not to Be...Self-Confident

It's no secret that some people, for whatever reason, are just naturally more self-assured than others. No matter how awkward the circumstances, these folks appear to be unflappable. Of course the reality is, while some may be more skilled than others at hiding insecurities, we all have them.

Lack of self-confidence tends to show up, even among the "unflappable," in efforts to control others, or the refusal to apologize or admit mistakes, like the guy who demanded, "Well, if I called the wrong number, why did you answer the phone?!"

The fallout from our insecurities can make those we love miserable and severely hamper our effectiveness among those we lead. Which begs the question: How can we elevate our self-confidence?

Psychologists write often and much on this topic, but this essay will briefly look at what the scriptures add to the discussion.

Not surprisingly, the Bible warns against depending on an upgrade of our physical appearance to improve our self-esteem. A diet or facelift may help in the short run, but it won't last ("Charm is deceptive and beauty is fleeting"– Proverbs 31:30). Exhibit A: Some of us guys have developed a "furniture" problem: our chest has dropped into our drawers. Sooner or later aging bodies deteriorate; so putting all our eggs in the appearance basket only sets us up for more insecurity.

Neither does the Bible advocate putting our hope in success to advance our sense of value. Fame and fortune come with no more guarantee of enduring than our physique. What's more, no matter our degree of success, there will always be others more successful, and when we meet one of these others, there goes our confidence ("Confidence placed in riches comes to nothing" – Proverbs 11:7).

So what does the Bible claim is a reliable source of enduring self-confidence? God. "The Lord will be your confidence and will keep your foot from being ensnared [by insecurity and low self-worth]" – Proverbs 3:26. How?

To begin with, Genesis records that we are made in God's image. That means we have dignity. How can we have an ape as a grandfather, as some claim, and have dignity? We can't. But we don't have an ape as a grandfather. The magnificent God made us in his image, and that gives us dignity.

Moreover, scientists agree that the complexity of our DNA blueprint eliminates any possibility of identical human beings. Why did God create each of us to be unique? According to scripture, he has a unique purpose for our life. Confidence stems from knowing that God brought each one of us into the world to fulfill a special assignment only we have the exclusive mix of gifts, abilities and talents to pull off.

But then too, self-confidence comes from knowing how much we are valued. Value is relative. I might value a painting at $25 because to me it looks like doodling. But somebody else, recognizing a masterpiece, buys it for $5 million. So what's the painting's value? $5 million. Value is determined by what somebody's willing to pay. The scriptures tell us that God thinks we're valuable enough to send his own Son to die in our place. The bottom line on our value is this: it's not what we might think that matters; it's what somebody's willing to pay. And Jesus says, "I paid it all. That's how valuable you are to me."

I'd like to suggest to you that confidence that endures through discouraging times when we may think, "I don't count for much," is found in the God who created us with dignity and a unique purpose and who died for us. It stands to reason then that the closer we get to him the more confidence we'll have, and the farther away from him we wander the less secure we're going to feel.

...serves as a trustworthy guide

Essay 46: A "GPS" for Life

"Trust in the Lord with all your heart and lean not on your own understanding, in all your ways acknowledge him, and he will make you paths straight" – Proverbs 3:5-6

In 2007, in the wake of hurricane Katrina, my wife and I, together with a team of other volunteers, spent a week in New Orleans helping restore several homes severely damaged in the storm and accompanying flood.

While in the "Big Easy," Ginny and I heard remarkable stories of men and women acting with uncommon courage during Katrina and the difficult days that followed. For example, Barry, a 30-something husband and father, held our group spellbound one evening as he told of smashing windows and clawing his way through rooftops to save 43 of his neighbors trapped in their homes by surging floodwaters. Barry also shared an enduring lesson drawn from his harrowing adventure. "You always want to wear your most spectacular shorts to bed," he advised. "I had my absolutely worst pair on the morning of the flood, and I ended up wearing nothing but those suckers the next five days, which I spent with 43 neighbors."

Another (and surely more practical) lesson I absorbed during our time in New Orleans was actually inspired by GPS technology. In an area where, post-flood, there were few street signs, you can imagine how valuable a GPS was… or should have been. Jack, Ginny's and my transportation while in New Orleans, had mounted a new Magellan Whizitron, or whatever, in his car. During our week in New Orleans it become clear that Jack was skeptical of this technology (Think: 2007, before GPS was commonplace). "This thing can't be accurate!" he would exclaim. Or, "I'm sure it's this other way." "Siri" proved flawless, but Jack struggled to believe her, nevertheless.

Afterwards, I chuckled as I remembered how Jack had made many wrong turns on the roads in New Orleans because of his doubts about GPS. But then it struck me that when trying to navigate the roads of life, I tend to have a similar problem. The Bible states that, like a heavenly GPS, God's Holy Spirit uses his Word to tell us, "Do this in your marriage, in your personal life, in your career. It's the straightest path to a successful life." But like Jack with his GPS, too often I say, "This can't be right." Or, "I like this other way better; it's much easier, and it's the direction the crowd's going." Rather than trusting God, as Proverbs 3:5-6 urges, I lean on my own understanding, inviting trouble of all sorts. You'd think I'd learn. Unfortunately, I continue to wrestle with this. How about you?

But here's something really cool about God that Magellan also illustrated. Each time Jack ignored Siri she quickly recalibrated; supplying a new set of instructions for what now was the optimum path to our destination. Siri never told Jack, "You idiot! Why didn't you listen to me?" Or, "You got yourself into this mess, Bub; now try getting out." Or, "Since you disregard me anyway, forget it. No more instructions."

And so it is, I've found, with God. No matter how many times I fail to trust him, he never washes his hands of me. As soon as I admit, "You were right, God. I'll listen now," he quickly provides a "recalibrated" set of instructions designed to "make my paths straight." Sure, our decisions to override God cause unnecessary pain and frustration. Obviously, it would be smart to trust him from the start. But even after years of "wrong turns," with God there's always reason to have hope.

PS A more recent GPS "tutorial": In December, 2014, I landed at Newark Airport confident I could follow Google Maps to West Point. To my chagrin, GPS failed utterly, leaving me for the next several hours wandering New Jersey's incomprehensible network of freeways. Here's the lesson: When it comes to life's final destination–where we'll spend eternity – it's a good idea to insure the reliability of what (or Whom) we're depending on for directions. Don't you agree?

...holds up under scrutiny

Essay 47: Reasons to Believe

"Why do you believe the Bible is true?" Christian apologist and author Josh McDowell writes in his book "The Last Christian Generation" that when he posed this question to a group of "solid Christian kids," the answer they came up with was, "We believe the Bible is true because we believe, because we have faith."

This answer, which in my experience is the one many adult Christians give as well, implies that the Bible isn't true for somebody unless they believe it. Hence, this: A young guy who knows what the Bible teaches about sex outside of marriage says, "I believe premarital sex is wrong, and I'm going to wait until I get married. But I can't force my view on other people."

Is the Bible true only for those who believe it's true? Or is it true no matter who believes it? Clearly, the Bible claims to be true. Proverbs 30:5, for instance, says, "Every word of God is flawless." But are there other reasons to believe that the Bible is trustworthy? What tests can we apply to the scriptures to assess their reliability? Following are three.

First, there's what might be called the facts test. Some argue that since the Bible has been translated hundreds of times, it can't be trustworthy. This ignores the fact that all translations are by scholars fluent in Hebrew and Greek who go back to manuscripts written in the original languages. There is also the fact of history and archaeology, both of which attest to the accuracy of the Bible. Then there's the fact of over 300 Old Testament prophecies of the coming of the Messiah that were fulfilled in Jesus.

Second, there's the practical living test. If we try to live in keeping with a certain worldview, but we keep bumping up against reality in painful ways, we can be certain something is wrong with our worldview.

You may remember Carl "Cosmos" Sagan. He held to a naturalistic – no god, it all came from nothing – worldview. One of the consequences of his worldview was that he was an animal rights advocate. Diagnosed with a rare blood disease, Sagan's only chance of survival was to undergo a procedure developed by research on animals. Though conflicted, he chose to undergo the treatment. He was plagued the rest of his life with the sense that what he had done was immoral.

Sagan's naturalism could not stand up to the test of practical living. Neither can Islam. Muslims deny women their basic rights. Neither can Hinduism. Hindus worship cows while millions starve. I submit to you that only the Christian faith, as described by the Bible, conforms to the way life works.

Finally, the Bible meets the purpose test. Humans can't live without a purpose, which is why many die soon after retiring. The Bible, on the other hand, asserts that we can know, honor and enjoy our Creator, the Being who is the perfect embodiment of all the qualities we deeply admire—courage, humility, kindness, mercy, forgiveness, etc. And it says that not only can we know this God personally, we can also partner with him to make a positive difference in the lives of others that will endure forever(!). What purpose could possibly give more satisfaction to the restless human heart?

Although these are but three of myriad tests pointing to the Bible's trustworthiness, proof beyond any doubt is not possible. After all, none of us witnessed the events that the scriptures record. Nevertheless, I invite you to consider whether the weight of these and the other reasons to believe don't remove all "reasonable" doubt. It has for me. This is why I can say that I don't think the Bible is true because I believe it, but that I believe the Bible because I'm convinced that it's true.

...may conflict with beliefs

Essay 48: Belief vs. Truth

*The 1998 film, "The Truman Show," aptly illustrates the gulf that can exist between belief and knowledge.

What is knowledge? While definitions vary, philoso-phers generally hold that knowledge is justified true belief, i.e., belief that agrees with the evidence.

In "The Truman Show" Truman Burbank was born and raised on a TV set, the star of his own show. He is com-pletely oblivious to this reality. Truman "believes" his life on Seahaven is real, not a scripted TV show. His belief does not, however, qualify as "knowledge" because it's unsup-ported by the evidence, i.e., the truth, as everybody else on the show and in the viewing audience clearly understands.

What is truth? Author Lael Arrington defines truth as a relationship between our words or ideas and reality. Truman's belief that he's a regular guy living a normal life, though he's sold on this idea, is still an untruth. Whether he can see it or not, whether what others tell him agrees with it or not, Truman's belief is false because it conflicts with reality.

In the film Truman begins to have doubts about what he's always believed. Lighting canisters fall out of the "sky." His "dad," supposedly dead, intrudes on the set and before he can be hustled away tries to warn Truman. Eventually, persuaded that he's being deceived and controlled, Truman escapes on a sailboat, which he sails to the edge of the watery set, literally poking a hole in the bubble of deceit that has surrounded his life.

We've probably all known people who unwittingly lived in deceit and illusion until one day they hit the wall of reality and faced a decision. They elected either to live according to knowledge (the truth), or they continued settling for an illusion. Truman chose the truth that set him free.

I'd like to suggest that you and I were born into a world of illusion. We come equipped with a conscience, which we sometimes violate, leaving us with a nagging sense of guilt. Since, however, this condition seems universal and few appear to be concerned about it, we assume there's nothing to worry about. Besides, if there is a day of reck-oning, we'll be okay, we believe, because our moral failures haven't been all that bad.

But do these beliefs correspond to the evidence? The ancient scriptures warn of a day of judgment on which all will be found guilty and sentenced to eternal punishment. Our only hope, it says, is in Jesus Christ. To those willing to put their trust in him, he offers the gift of forgiveness on the basis of his death in payment for our moral failures.

Some say, "I don't believe that, and neither do most other people." But, as we noted with Truman, if our beliefs are contrary to the evidence, they are not true, no matter how convinced of them we may be or who agrees with us.

So are the scriptures truth or untruth, knowledge or fiction, reality or myth? The Bible book of Proverbs offers this word of counsel, "The heart of the discerning acquires knowledge; the ears of the wise seek it out" (18:15). He reminds us that wise people seek out the truth for them-selves, rather than simply taking the word of someone else. And if it turns out that the evidence supports the trustwor-thiness of the Bible, then of course there's a decision to make: "Do I adjust my course as necessary to live according to knowledge and be free, or do I settle for illusion, for living in deception and control?"

*Adapted from an article by Lael Arrington

...is often ignored in money matters

Essay 49: The Truth about Money

*After 6 years of making do with a 900-square-foot home, Mark and Jill Thompson were ready to move into a larger house and start a family. It's something they had saved for since the day they were married. Following the advice of a friend, they arranged a meeting with Jay, a mortgage broker.

Jay showed the Thompsons what they could qualify for with their credit rating and a product that would lock them in at 3% with a point a year rise for the next 5 years. With this product, Jay assured them, they could get twice the house for half the money they had saved for a down payment. What's more they could take the $15,000 that they didn't put down and invest it in the market, which, according to Jay, typically earns 4 to 6% more than what they would pay on the mortgage. And in the event that money got tight, they could always sell the house and downsize.

Is stretching for more the right thing to do? On the one hand, we don't want to do something dumb, something that would rob us of peace of mind and even get us into debt that might take years to climb out of. On the other hand, we don't want to play it too close to the vest and miss out on our dream. This can be a gut-wrenching decision. A lot of people live with this tension because they are unsure of the truth about money.

What is the truth about money, and where do we find this truth? At first glance there might seem to be hundreds, if not thousands, of "truth sources" to choose from. I'd like to suggest however that there are really only two choices: the world, i.e., the opinions and assertions of men that we glean primarily from the media, and the Bible.

What does the world say is true about money? Here are a few examples: You only go around once so it's best to take a debt and live life with the gusto we deserve. If things get tight, as Jay said, we can always sell and get out of debt. Our next purchase will bring us happiness.

The scriptures give us an entirely different perspective on money. For instance, Proverbs 22:27 tells us that, "If you have no money to pay, even your bed will be taken from you." Preoccupied with thoughts of what they want, many borrowers fail to consider the worst that could happen. So this proverb reminds us where borrowing can take us. And since we don't like to be told what to do or what not to do, instead of giving us a "don't do this," this verse paints a vivid picture of what today we would call "foreclosure" and "repossession."

He's saying, "Before you borrow think about this: When you can't pay your bills, your very bed, the most private area of your home, the place where you snuggle with your spouse and lay your head to rest, your last bastion of peace can be taken from you."

One of the errors the world makes in its understanding of money is that it presupposes something will happen, usually something good, that we have no control over whatever. Proverbs 13:10 gives us the antidote to presumption: "Arrogance [presumption] leads to nothing but strife, but wisdom is with those who receive counsel." He advises that we talk to people who have been where we are contemplating going, and that we ask if in their opinion we are acting presumptuously.

And here's a thought: We might want to seek out someone whose counsel is based on the Bible's perspective on money, which clearly has the ring of truth, rather than the world's perspective, which often is little more than conjecture.

*With lots of help from "The Truth about Money Lies" by Russ Crosson

...is likely to clash with expectations

Essay 50: Because Life Is Not Always as It Seems

Have you heard the story of the wise old Chinese woodcutter who long ago lived on the troubled Mongolian border?

One day his favorite horse, a beautiful white mare, ran away and ended up on the wrong side of the border, where she was seized by the enemy. The woodcutter's friends all came to commiserate with him over this bad news.

"How do you know it's bad news?" he asked. "It might be good news."

A week later, the mare returned...alongside a beautiful stallion. The man's friends came again, this time to congratulate him on the good news of this new addition to his herd.

"How do you know it's good news?" he asked. "It might be bad news."

The next day, the woodcutter's only son decided to try the stallion. It threw him, and he broke his leg. The friends paid another visit. "We're so sorry about this bad news," they said.

To which the man replied, "How do you know it's bad news? It might be good news."

Within a month war broke out between China and Mongolia. Chinese recruiters came through the area, pressing all the young men into the army. They all perished, except for the woodcutter's son. He couldn't go off to war because–you guessed it–his leg was broken.

"You see," the wise old woodcutter told his friends, "the things you considered good were actually bad, and the things that seemed bad were actually good."

Isn't that the way life is? So often what's good and what's bad is counterintuitive. Take for instance the businessman who dedicates his life to providing his family with all the advantages that money can buy–the 10,000-square-foot house, Mediterranean cruises, private schools – only to lose his family because they needed him more than the so-called advantages, and he was seldom available.

Wouldn't it be terrific if there were a way to know what's truly important in life without going through the agony of trial and error? Enter Proverbs 8:35: "Whoever finds wisdom finds life and receives favor from the Lord." If there is a Master Designer, it stands to reason that he understands how his creation works – what's good and what only appears to be good. The message of Proverb 8:35 is not only that there is such a Designer, but also that he gladly offers us his wisdom, i.e., his unique and often "contrary to our expectations" perspective on life.

For example, conventional thinking says, "I have to take care of number one because if others win, that means I lose." Jesus, on the other hand, said that we gain by losing ("For whoever desires to save his life will lose it, but whoever loses his life for my sake will save it"). So which philosophy, when applied, actually works? Remember Zig Ziglar? A brilliant leader, one of his best-known quotes is, "You can have anything you want in life, if you help enough other people get what they want out of life." Following Jesus' philosophy of putting others first, Ziglar literally built an empire from nothing.

Conventional wisdom also holds that you fight your way to the top of the organization, and once there "you run the show"–you know, freely express your anger and criticism, make yourself the focus of every task, that kind of thing. But Jesus said, "Whoever wants to be great will be the servant of all." By the way, have you noticed all the emphasis by secular leadership gurus nowadays on being a humble, self-effacing leader? They observed that Jesus' way works and the other doesn't.

Life is not always as it seems. Or, as John Maxwell puts it: "The worst thing that could happen to you today could lead to the best thing that happens tomorrow." I would argue therefore that staying tuned in to what the Designer has said makes perfect sense.

...claims to be authoritative

Essay 51: To Bet Your Life

"Be careful how you think; your life is shaped by your thoughts" – Proverbs 4:23

Growing up, we learned about the tooth fairy, Santa Clause and the Easter bunny. These fables are part of American culture and of course generally harmless. There are, however, other myths we may have absorbed from the culture that can be hazardous to our health and happiness.

Take for example the idea that it doesn't matter what we believe as long as we're sincere. Sounds so broadminded and tolerant. You know, different strokes for different folks. You believe this, I believe that, and everything's cool. Right?

Umm, not so fast. Some beliefs are contradictory – I mean, Elvis is either still alive or he isn't. So somebody's got to be believing the wrong stuff about Elvis. And my thesis here is when our beliefs are faulty, no matter how sincere we may be, the results, unlike with the tooth fairy, can be quite serious, even ruinous.

The thing that makes what we believe so decisive, as Proverbs 4:23 points out, is that our beliefs shape our behavior. Why do we go to a doctor when we're sick? We're motivated by the belief that an MD can help us feel better. When at a restaurant, we select something off the menu because we believe it's going to taste good. The fact is there's a belief behind pretty much every conscious action we take.

Okay. So what? Here's the problem: Our beliefs, even when "wrong," govern our actions. For instance, if I believe that when in a group I never have anything important to say, I'll keep silent, though I may have the very input needed to reach the best decision. If I believe I'm unlovable, I'll behave in an unlovable way. If I believe, as a woman who lay "dead" on a surgical table for 45 minutes told Dr. Oz she does, that, based on her experience, what we all can expect at death is a euphoric sense of peace, then it's doubtful I'll be concerned, as one who has broken God's law, about finding a way to avoid his righteous judgment.

Hence, the million-dollar question: What's the standard by which we determine what to believe? Or to put it another way, what's our authority for how we live our life?

It occurs to me that there are really only a couple possible options. One: Believe essentially what the culture tells us, even though what it tell us frequently changes. Take for instance Dr. Spock's book on childcare. All 77 million of us boomers were brought up on "Baby and Childcare," in which the good doctor mixed a little Freud with the childcare philosophy the "Greatest Generation" was raised on. Several years ago, however, Dr. Spock held a press conference to say, "Oops, I was wrong. I'm sorry. Never mind." And we're going, "Yeah, thanks a lot, doc. Now that I'm dysfunctional it's a little late."

One option then is to let the culture decide what we believe. I'd say this option is questionable at best. What's the other possibility? We can go with transcendent revelation, truth communicated to man by a God who is bound by his nature to tell the truth.

If only there were such a thing, you say. It's no secret that the scriptures throughout claim to tell the truth. Of course, each person owes it to him or her self to carefully examine the evidence supporting this claim, but I would argue that the evidence has already held up against the closest of scrutiny by the greatest of skeptics, many of whom ended up Christ-followers – author and educator C.S. Lewis, physician-geneticist Francis Collins, journalist-author Malcolm Muggeridge, to name a few.

So when it comes to the basis for our beliefs and behavior, I would suggest that there are these two options, and that we have to decide which is reliable...and that we bet our life on what we choose.

...is found through diligent effort

Essay 52: Kings Reveal/God Conceals

"It is the glory of God to conceal a matter; to search out a matter is the glory of kings" – Proverbs 25:2

Eight hundred years ago last week, at Runnymede, England, King John, under duress, signed the Magna Carta guaranteeing his people certain freedoms as a means of protecting them from the arbitrary authority of a despot. This document, first drafted by the Archbishop of Canterbury, reflects the biblical principle of legal and human rights. In ordaining the spheres of human authority it's clear that God intended rule to be for the protection of the people, not for the pleasure of the king.

To insure justice for those under his authority, before making a judgment a noble ruler will carefully investigate, "search out a matter" in the words of Proverbs 25:2, in order to expose the truth. To those of us steeped in the individual freedoms guaranteed by the Declaration of Independence and the Constitution (the two documents directly inspired by the Magna Carta) this comes as no surprise. What may surprise, however, is the assertion in Proverbs 25:2 that rather than "revealment," as with kings, God is into concealment.

This may explain why perceptions of what God is like run the gamut. Some say he's an old-fashioned, grandfather sort of guy who means well but is too weak and out of touch with modern man to be of any real help. Others are convinced that God is an anti-fun, cosmic killjoy. Still others tell us he's an absentee creator too busy for personal involvement with his creation. Why all the different under-standings of God? Maybe it's because he's chosen to conceal himself.

What if you and I decide, "Instead of depending on the opinions of others, I want to discover for myself what God is like"? Is this possible? Will God make himself known? The Bible says he will, but only to the resolute: "If you search for it like a prospector panning for gold, like an adventurer on a treasure hunt, believe me, before you know it you'll have come upon the knowledge of God" (Proverbs 2:4-5). God promises to disclose himself to those determined to know him.

Sometimes people say, "I tried reading the Bible once, but it just didn't make sense, so I gave up." No question, com-prehending the scriptures can be challenging. It's almost as though God designed it that way to discourage all but those who bring to the "hunt" a resolve not to be denied. Is it worth the effort? I would contend that it is. Allow me to cite a for instance why.

Most people know enough about the 10 Commandments to agree (and be haunted by the notion) that they prescribe a model of behavior that we should practice but often don't. "So what now?" we ask. "How do I make peace with God and rid myself of this guilt?" Responses to this question vary. They include living a better life the next time around, doing enough good to cancel out the bad, and performing acts of penance. Granted, these "solutions" may bury our shame for a while, but the guilt feelings have a nasty habit of res-urrecting themselves.

The Bible's answer? It's what we would least expect. God has concealed this matter so thoroughly from our "there ain't no free lunch" mentality that only a steadfast "mining" of his word reveals it. Who would have ever fathomed the possibility that instead of us somehow satisfying God's justice through appeasement, as all manmade religions attempt to do, God satisfied it himself by exacting judgment on his own Son? The Bible declares that it's all by grace: that forgiveness and freedom from guilt come freely through trusting that Jesus paid for our sins. So, is discovering this and the other nuggets God has hidden in the scriptures worth the effort? You be the judge.

Category 4

In my opinion, if you are in a state of hopelessness then any god worth being called a god would help you before reaching rock bottom and without being prayed to and asked or begged for help. "
– Daniel Metivier (atheist)

For God so loved the world that he gave his one and only Son, that whoever believes in him shall not perish but have eternal life. – Jesus Christ
(The Gospel of John: 3:16)

Essays 53-60:

Hope, peace and security are found in...

...understanding God's character

Essay 53: The Power of a Name

What's in a person's name? Maybe nothing more than the identity of their dad or mom's favorite film star. On the other hand, a name may reflect the character qualities parents hope to see mirrored one day in their child.

There's a reason we probably don't know anybody named Judas. Who's going to saddle their son with a handle that conjures up thoughts of cowardice and treachery? On the other hand, many of us likely named our son or daughter after someone with that same name whose character we admire. I find it interesting that a name and a set of character qualities can be so intertwined in our thoughts that the two are almost inseparable. Mention Mother Teresa, Abraham Lincoln, Adolph Hitler, Billy Graham, Osama bin Laden, and character comes immediately into play. Obviously there's something unusual going on here.

This leads us to a proverb in the Bible that intersects with this name/character-quality association thing.

Proverb 18:10 says, "The name of the Lord is a strong tower; the righteous run to it and are safe." This verse claims that what the ancient scriptures reveal about God's "name" gives insight into his character. The argument here is that this insight makes it unreasonable, when depending on God for our present and future, to feel anything less than completely secure. To illustrate this security he compares it to what soldiers feel when engaging the enemy from an impregnable fortress.

Now I'm aware not everyone will agree that Proverbs 18:10 is relevant. Why would I be interested in God as a source of security when in every circumstance I've found my own resourcefulness sufficient to keep me calm, cool and collected? I understand this point of view. Actually I shared it for a number of years. Then I discovered that, at least for me, there are things in life, like broken career dreams, difficult marital issues, the death of a parent, strong-willed kids, financial struggles, the prospect of my own death, etc., that made the idea of a "tower" to run to for security, consolation and some perspective pretty compelling.

So what names in the Bible identify God as a source of security? Let me cite a couple of the many. In Psalm 23, David is reflecting on how God has helped him through times of discouragement, times of confusion, times when he found himself in a valley of deep darkness needing protection. David uses the name "God is my Shepherd" to illustrate how in his distress God's persistent, loving protection was like that of a good shepherd who knows the right paths on which to bring the sheep safely home. That's security.

The Bible records that during Israel's exodus from Egypt Moses returned from meeting with God to find the people reveling and worshiping an idol. God's judgment was swift, many perished. Moses feared what this blatant disrespect for God would mean for the nation long term considering they were in a desert, dependent on God for everything, even directions to where they were going. Not well acquainted with God's character at this point, Moses said, "God, help me know you better." God did. According to the record, God said, "Moses, my name is Jehovah, and that name means I'm a God who punishes evildoers, but who also is gracious, loving, patient and forgiving. Moses found in God's name the security he needed to go on.

The good news is "The name of the Lord is a strong tower." The bad news is only the righteous will find refuge in this tower. The worse news is nobody fits the Bible's description of righteous. But the best news of all is that God is gracious, which is where another of his names comes into sharp focus. The angel said to Joseph, "You will call his name Jesus [God is salvation] because he will save his people from their sins."

...owning God's evaluation

Essay 54: Overcoming Fear of Rejection

"The fear of human opinion disables; trusting in God protects you from that" – Proverbs 29:15

Successful, confident people give the appearance of living without fear. I would argue, however, that there's one fear that frequently plagues even the most successful and seemingly confident among us. I'm talking about the fear of rejection, which Proverbs 29:25 warns, "disables."

Ever find yourself wearing a mask and acting out the role of "I've got it all together"? Who hasn't? Fearful of exposing our weaknesses, we know what it is to play it close to the vest, act defensively, fake it.

Fear of rejection can cause us to avoid confrontation at all costs. We may not speak up even to make our needs known, resulting in passive-aggressive behavior.

Then there's the other stuff we tend to do to win others' approval. You know, like wearing sport shirts with a tiny logo that doubles the price, or sinking a fortune into a "muscle" car, or owning a house that looks more like a hotel than a home. Or maybe we've become a workaholic because we think it pleases somebody, or a namedropper, or we belong to a certain country club. As somebody quipped, people spend money they don't have to buy stuff they don't need to impress people they don't even like. Why? Because fearing rejection, we're determined to prove that we are somebody.

Is there an antidote to this disabling fear? Several possibilities showed up in my web search. One recommendation is that we build up a tolerance to rejection by repeatedly putting ourselves in positions where we're likely to experience the rotten feeling that comes with each new failure. Eventually, we're assured, we'll develop insensitivity to rejection and become a stronger person. Well, maybe.

Another well-meaning individual counsels that whenever we begin to feel unsure of ourselves, we should use that fear as fuel to move us forward. This is the "stop being a wuss and just deal with it" technique.

Then there's the more analytical approach. We list our irrational fears, being careful to put them in order from least to most fearful. Beginning with the least paralyzing situation, we take an action step that addresses our fear. Then, after rewarding ourselves in some way for our success, we repeat this process.

With all due respect to these web contributors, I'd like to offer what I believe is a simpler and more effective way to conquer the fear of rejection, namely, the one suggested in Proverbs 29:25: put our trust in God. How does that help? Studies have shown that more than anything else our self-esteem is shaped by what we believe the most important person in our life thinks about us.

So let me ask you, what value do you think God places on you and me? Value, of course, is relative. For example, a painting that to me looks like it might be worth maybe $25, an art connoisseur might pay a million bucks for. What's the painting's value? A million bucks. You see, in the matter of value, it's not what we might think that matters; rather, it's what somebody's willing to pay.

So again the question, what value does God place on us? The Bible says that there is only one person we will never have to convince that we are good enough for him to love us. He's the same one who proved his love by dying for us. Jesus said, "I paid it all for you. That's how valuable you are to me."

Here's the bottom line if we believe the proverb: When we make Jesus Christ the most important person in our life and begin to understand that he really does love us unconditionally, we're set free to drop the mask and live a more authentic and fulfilling life.

...accepting God's purpose for suffering

Essay 55: If God Is Good, Why Suffering?

Years ago, I built a friendship with Calvin Austin, a man I grew to greatly admire. Calvin possessed the rare combination of brilliance and humility. One of the most successful and highly regarded physicians in that part of Arkansas, I never saw him use his influence to try to ram through his viewpoint. If, on the other hand, someone was needed to mop floors, mow grass, or clean toilets, or maybe to pay a widow's overdue mortgage or stock her empty refrigerator, you could count on Calvin.

A devoted Christ follower, Dr. Austin was a loving husband, father and grandfather, a caring employer and, although a physician in high demand, a sterling example of what it means to balance family and career responsibilities. If ethical behavior guaranteed good fortune, Calvin would certainly have qualified. Yet, in his 60s he contracted Lou Gehrig's disease, and, after several years of intense suffering, he passed away.

Human suffering, especially when it involves virtuous people or innocent children (or us), naturally gives rise to the question: If God is good, why is there suffering? The skeptic seizes upon the reality of suffering to dismiss the Bible view of an all-powerful and loving God, reasoning that, "If God loves us, he must not be all-powerful or else he could stop all suffering," or, "If God is all-powerful and could stop suffering but doesn't, he must not be loving."

I would like to suggest a third possibility. In chapter 16 of the Bible book of Proverbs, Israel's King Solomon writes this: "In his heart a man plans his course, but the Lord determines his steps" (v. 9). What has this to do with the apparent contradiction between a good God and human suffering? Allow me to explain.

The Bible presents God as the highest and greatest of all beings, who works within human history to achieve his purpose, sometimes by the laws of nature, other times by spectacular miracle. Sometimes by human agents, other times without them. My point is scripture claims that God is sovereign, that within his creation whatever he says goes...with one exception.

While God controls everything, the Bible makes it clear that he does not manipulate people like marionettes. He has given us the freewill to make our own decisions, and he holds us responsible for our choices. The Bible's perspective is that all human suffering is ultimately linked in some way to man's evil choices. That's the bad news. The good news is that because God is sovereign he's able to overrule man's evil actions to accomplish his perfect purposes.

The scriptures are filled with illustrations of this. For instance, Joseph's brothers hatched a plan to get rid of their brother, but God directed their steps to sell him into Egypt, where he saved them all from starvation. In the New Testament, the Jewish religious leaders hatched their plan to rid themselves of the troublesome carpenter turned itinerant preacher, but God determined to use their murderous designs to fulfill his plan to lay on his Son the guilt and penalty of the world's sins and provide forgiveness for the human race.

It would seem then that when our world collapses into pain and suffering, we have a choice to react in one of two ways. We can resist God, grumble, and accuse him of being unkind, impotent or both, and end up with a tension headache, a knot of bitterness in the pit of our stomach, and possibly an ulcer or heart attack. Or we can elect to believe that living in an imperfect world includes suffering, but that a loving, all-powerful, sovereign God somehow uses even suffering to work out his good purpose. My friend Calvin adopted the latter perspective, and as a result he found inner peace and joy in the midst of his pain.

...cheering the heart with the gospel

Essay 56: Finally, Some Good News!

"A cheerful heart is good medicine, but a crushed spirit saps a person's strength"-Proverbs 17:22

Here's a sample of what today's Wall Street Journal considers newsworthy. The DOW was down yesterday 166 points. The Army is trying to figure out why Spc. Ivan Lopez killed three colleagues and injured 16 others before taking his own life in the latest Fort Hood shooting spree.

The search continues for Malaysia Airlines Flight 370 and for an explanation of the apparent loss of 239 passengers and crew. Pro-Russia unrest swells in eastern Ukraine, as Vladimir Putin appears to be following his Crimea script of intimidation and political meddling. Hmm...not real encouraging stuff there.

Let's see what's happening with some of the polls. According to Gallop, 25% of U.S. workers are either un- or under-employed and 43% of Americans report that they are struggling. RealClearPolitics has Congress' approval rating at 13% with 79% disapproving. Yikes!

Then there's our national debt crisis: $17 trillion and counting, the threat to our very existence posed by rogue nations and various other terrorist organizations, not to mention personal issues, such as health, finances, strained relationships, etc. Wow! It's not hard to understand why we might need some medicine in the form of good news to cheer our hearts lest "a crushed spirit sap our strength."

The good news I'd like to offer for your consideration is this, "For God so loved the world that he gave his one and only Son, that whoever believes in him shall not perish but have eternal life."

I find in this verse four reasons to smile. One, as to the matter of a friendship between God and us, it says God cared enough to make the first move. The scriptures explain that nobody is looking for God, not really. To satisfy our natural yearning to recognize something greater than ourselves or maybe to ease our guilt, we might turn to a creed or to a list of dos and don'ts that offer a way to earn heaven, but to humbly seek to connect with Jehovah God, who tenders heaven as a free gift, it says we're not interested in that. So if we are to know God, he had to make the first move, and he did. That's good news!

Two, when I think about how God might feel toward mankind, what comes to mind is indifference or maybe hatred. After all, the Bible confirms that as human beings our natural bent is to refuse to give the Creator more than a tip of the hat. Why shouldn't he feel indifference or hatred toward us? But it says he "loved" us...to the unimaginable degree that he sacrificed his Son for us. That's good news!

Three, our part in establishing this friendship is faith – "whoever 'believes' in him." He could have demanded that we keep the Ten Commandments. Have you ever taken anything that wasn't yours? Lusted after another person or worse? Told a lie? You too, huh? We're all guilty. The fact that our friendship with God hinges on faith, not on performance, that's good news.

Finally, there's the eternal life part – "shall not perish but have 'eternal life,'" which the scriptures define as both quantity and quality of life. Heaven verses hell, later (and forever), but right now, peace of mind, purpose, freedom from fear, and God's power for change. I'd say that's good news, too.

John 3:16 summarizes what the Bible calls the gospel (literally, "good news"). Here then is a suggestion: Every day, to keep what's happening in the world from crushing our spirit and sapping our strength, we cheer our heart (and maybe somebody else's heart, too) with the good medicine of the gospel.

...facing and forgiving hurts

Essay 57: Recovering from Life's Hurts

"An angry man starts fights and gets into all kinds of trouble" – Proverbs 29:22

People hurt people. It's a fact. Unintentionally–and maybe every now and then on purpose–we hurt others, and they hurt us. How we process that hurt can deeply affect our happiness in life. Mishandled hurt morphs into anger and resentment, emotions that as Proverbs 29:22 reminds us get us into troubles of all kinds.

For insight into how to recover from hurt, who better to look at than the biblical figure Job? Who has had more hurt inflicted on him than Job? In one day he lost his vast wealth, all 10 of his kids were killed, his wife turned against him, and he was afflicted with an excruciating, incurable disease. Then his friends showed up and instead of offering consolation they said, "It's all your fault." Job had every reason to be resentful, but it says he worked through his pain and got on with his life. How'd he do that?

He started by admitting his hurt: "If my misery could be weighed, if you could pile the whole bitter load on the scales, it would be heavier than all the sand of the sea!" In other words, he said, "God has dumped the whole works on me."

When we have painful things in our past – a parent's abuse or absence, a former spouse's unfaithfulness, a deserved promotion we never got – sometimes we say, "I just want to forget about it." But have you noticed how these things keep resurrecting themselves? Little incidents trigger stuff we thought was buried, and the searing pain returns. On the other hand, as somebody said, revealing the feeling is the beginning of healing.

So Job's attitude is, "I don't like it; it's unfair; the situation stinks; and I'm PO'ed...with you, God." He told God exactly how he felt. Ever try that? "But I don't want to hurt God's feelings. Besides, he might fry me with a thunderbolt." He didn't fry Job. Hey, God was aware of Job's feelings as soon as he got angry. And God understood. Somebody says, "Where were you, God, when my son died?" God says, "The same place I was when my Son died on a cross." God knows about hurt and he invites us to share our pain with him.

Another thing Job did, he forgave his offenders. His so-called friends misunderstood him, criticized him and falsely accused him. We understand how that hurts. Job had every right to resent these guys. But the turnaround in his life didn't come until he gave up this right. He even prays for their success.

You know, sometimes the hurt can run so deep we think, "There's no way I can ever forgive them." I'm sure some of us have been there. Fortunately, Jesus says, "I can help you with that." The one who forgave those who crucified him offers us his divine power to let go of the feeling that "but they owe me."

Finally, we see from Job's story that after we admit the pain and let God fill us with forgiveness, we can face the world again. I've found, as you may have, that a deep hurt can lead to an overwhelming urge to never let down our guard again lest somebody take advantage of us. And we can withdraw into a shell. But Job's example teaches us that we've got to stop letting what happened in the past define us as a victim, start facing the future, and get on with living.

In the final chapter of Job's bio it says, "God blessed the last part of Job's life even more than he had blessed the first!" The memories faded and the pain along with them, and the rest of Job's life turned out to be the best of his life. God says it can be that way for anybody who's willing to partner with him in letting go of past hurts.

...living in partnership with God

Essay 58: Maintaining a Positive Attitude

"A cheerful disposition is good for your health; gloom and doom leave you bone-tired" – Proverbs 17:22

Would you agree that attitude drives success in life?

Lou Holtz, former premier football coach, today is a highly sought after motivational speaker who inspires people well beyond the realm of sports. Such a successful man surely started out with some kind of "right stuff" giving him a leg up on the rest of us, right? Wrong. Holtz came from a broken family. He stumbled out of life's starting blocks like many of us did. Yet, he became a remarkable person. How come? He attributes his success to maintaining a positive attitude. "Life," he says, "is 10% what happens to you and 90% how you respond to it."

Playing contrarian for a moment, even if Holtz' arithmetic is correct, the 10% of life that's about circumstances represents some daunting realities.

Centuries ago, King Solomon, with his unlimited wealth and power, set out to uncover life's purpose. He tried sex, drugs, work, education, and much more. In the opening section of the Bible book of Ecclesiastes, Solomon's journal, he records his findings: there is nothing in this world that truly satisfies. When all is said and done, he writes, life is meaningless, boring and full of pain.

In the film City Slickers there's a "Facts of Life" scene where Mitch (Billy Crystal) tells his son's class to enjoy their childhood because it's all downhill from there. My guess is part of what makes this clip so funny is that, like Mitch, we can all identify with it.

Recently, I watched via YouTube quarterback Tom Brady's appearance six years ago on "60 Minutes." Given Brady's money and fame, interviewer Steve Kroft is surprised to hear this man who seems to have it all, including three Super Bowl rings, lament, "There's got to be more than this."

No matter the size of our job, house or bank account, when the lights are turned off at night and we face reality, it's natural to wonder, "Is this all there is?"

One guy, clinging to the hope that his existence counted for something, wrote, "...my journey through the darkness... is an adventure filled with suspense–and cruelty and meaninglessness. And though I do not know what is ahead, never fear, I am on my way!....Even as I swallow my tranquilizers, rush to my psychiatrist, take that extra drink, and endure my third divorce...–I still say there is hope!"

Where? Solomon, the wisest of men, asserts that hope is a pipe dream, that there is no ultimate meaning to this crummy existence.

So, how does anybody maintain a positive attitude? I suppose we can dream, as some do, that we're on the brink of a great happening that will change everything. The ancient scriptures suggest that there's a better way. As his journal unfolds, Solomon weaves into the text a viewpoint left out of his earlier conclusion: the perspective of life in partnership with God. He says that with God in the picture, boredom, emptiness and despair give way to transcendent meaning and hope.

Back to Lou Holtz. One author I read guessed that Holtz' positive outlook is due to his "spiritual inclinations." He's right. I'm acquainted with the man who helped Holtz become a Christ-follower.

Jesus said, "I came that you might have a rich and satisfying life." And as far as death is concerned, the Bible portrays it as a veil through which the believer passes into a mind-blowing eternity spent with God. My experience is that through trusting the promises in the Bible, and with God's help, we can face life's struggles and hurts with the cheerful disposition Proverbs 17:22 talks about.

...choosing to relish each moment

Essay 59: "He Has Made Everything Beautiful in It's Time"

"A man's steps are directed by the Lord. How then can anyone understand his own way?" – Proverbs 20:24

*It's been a decade now since the young couple buried his parents and their only child, Abigail, victims of a fiery private plane crash here in Tulsa. The pilot, Rick, and his wife Debbie, both acquaintances of mine, were off to vacation in Canada. The first leg of their journey would take them to Missouri to return Abigail, their weekend guest, to her parents. Shortly after takeoff, Rick radioed the tower about an engine problem and their emergency return to the airfield. Tragically, moments later the Cessna dropped from the sky.

In his early fifties, Rick had only recently retired. His son and daughter-in-law must have eagerly anticipated the greater flexibility these devoted grandparents would now have to love on their family. How shocking for them to learn that their dream had been dashed and their family members snatched away.

"This couple did so much volunteer work," the general manager of Rick and Debbie's tennis club was quoted as saying. "Whatever we do to honor their memory won't do justice to the type of people they were." Hundreds attended their funeral. Why were these extraordinary folks taken in their prime? And what about little Abby, whose life had only begun?

And, while we're on the subject of life's calamities, what about all the innocent victims of terrorism, many of them children? And what about war hero Chris Kyle, survivor of four combat tours who was murdered by a fellow US

soldier? And what about a young Jewish carpenter crucified for healing the sick and offering forgiveness and eternal
life? And what about___? You fill in the blank.

Is there any sense at all to be made of such appalling,
often totally unexpected events? I'd like to suggest to you a
point of view offered in the Bible book of Ecclesiastes that
I've found helpful in gaining some perspective on this.

A well-known passage in Ecclesiastes, popularized years
ago by songwriter Bob Dylan, notes that God has a perfect
timetable and season for everything that enters our lives,
both good and evil: "There is a time for everything, and a
season for every activity under heaven: a time to be born
and a time to die, a time to plant and a time to uproot, a time
to kill and a time to heal, a time to tear down and a time to
build, a time to weep and a time to laugh…"

Ecclesiastes advises that since only God knows how long
each of these seasons of life will last, the wise man, rather
than taking what he has for granted and pining for more,
will set his mind to enjoy his life, relishing each moment
while he has it. Or, as a friend who recently lost his wife to
cancer put it, "The wise man will stay in the moment and
take nothing for granted."

Behind all of life's obscurities, Ecclesiastes adds, the
God who has everything carefully choreographed, is mys-
teriously working good: "He has made everything beautiful
in its time. He has also set eternity in the hearts of men;
yet they cannot fathom what God has done from beginning
to end."

Though life may career out of control, sometimes
with catastrophic results, each day brings new hope and
opportunities, along with new and frequently incomprehensible challenges. But the one who believes that God
is there, accomplishing his perfect plan right on schedule
and with our best interest at heart, as the Bible assures
us he is, is able to find hope and peace of mind. God's plan

is unfathomable–we can't really understand it–but it's also "beautiful in its time."

*In conjunction with thoughts from Dwight Hill

...realizing that nothing is impossible with God

Essay 60: Embracing a "Beyond Z" Perspective

"The horses are prepared for battle, but the victory belongs to the Lord" – Proverbs 21:31

Are you in a battle? It could be a relationship battle. You know, you have a colleague, and in meetings no matter what side of an issue you're on he or she is always stridently opposed. Or maybe your problem is a chronically complaining relative. You can't stand being around them, but they'll be at the family reunion again this year, and you're dreading it.

It might be a health battle. Or maybe we're discouraged because the old body just doesn't work as well as it once did. Or maybe a loved one is ill or even has died, and our battle is drawn along those lines.

Of course, with the weak economy of the past several years, our battle might be financial – we're approaching retirement, and our resources are inadequate; our organization is on the brink of failure; or we're upside down on our house. Whatever the particulars, we're afraid the proverbial wolf is not far from the door.

Potential battles are legion. We all face them, and my guess is, despite our best efforts, we're losing ground in some of them. That's the bad news. The good news is Proverbs 21:31 offers hope for those in "combat." But before we examine this hope, first a word of wisdom from writer and cartoonist Dr. Seuss.

In his book "On Beyond Zebra" the good doctor exhorts a young friend, Conrad Cornelius o'Donald o'Dell, who we're told is just learning to spell, to avoid the rut of limiting his alphabet to A-Z. It's only in going beyond Z, Dr. Seuss declares, that Conrad can explore the exhilarating world of, among other "letters," YUZZ, used of course to spell Yuzz-a-ma-Tuzz, and HUMPF, as in Humpf-Humpf-a-Dumpfer.

"I tried hard," Dr. Seuss explains, "to tell young Conrad Cornelius o'Donald o'Dell a few brand-new wonderful words he might spell. I led him around and I tried hard to show there are things beyond Z that most people don't know. I took him past Zebra. As far as I could. And I think, perhaps, I did him some good.... Because finally he said, 'This is really great stuff! And I guess the old alphabet ISN'T enough!' NOW the letters he uses are something to see! Most people "still" stop at the Z... "But not HE!""

The battles you and I are fighting...and perhaps losing, I'd like to suggest that a limited, A-Z perspective could be hampering our efforts to win.

Allow me to illustrate from the Christmas story in the scriptures. You remember. An angel says to Mary, "You're going to have a baby." And she says, "Big problem. I'm a virgin." Mary was thinking in A-Z terms. In an A-Z world women don't have babies without a man's involvement. So the angel helped Mary to understand that there's a "beyond Z" world where "nothing is impossible," because of God.

Hence, the hope to which Proverbs 21:31 directs our attention. It's true that in an A-Z world there are folks we're never going to get along with. And in an A-Z world there are physical and financial crises and many other battles that we're not going to win. So coping with these unhappy circumstances is the best we can hope for in an A-Z world. But in God's "beyond Z" world he promises not coping, but victory.

Now the Proverb states that it's up to us to "prepare the horses for battle." In other words, we must make the effort to be friendly with thorny folks, to maintain a positive outlook in the face of declining health, to provide for our family, etc.–you know, as best we can, do the A-Z stuff. But the victory, he says, comes through maintaining a "beyond Z" perspective, i.e., trusting in the God of the impossible to seal the deal.

In need of a "beyond Z" perspective? No time like the present to ask God for one.

BLESSED are those who find WISDOM, those who gain UNDERSTANDING, for she is MORE PROFITABLE than silver and yields BETTER RETURNS than gold. She is MORE PRECIOUS than rubies; NOTHING you desire CAN COMPARE with her. LONG LIFE is in her right hand; in her left hand are RICHES and HONOR. Her ways are PLEASANT ways, and all her paths are PEACE. She is a TREE OF LIFE to those who take hold of her; those who hold her fast will be BLESSED.

___

Proverbs 3:13-18

Appendix A

My Faith Story

I devoted my life as a young adult to the pursuit of the Great American Dream. Growing up somehow convinced that I wasn't as valued as those with money, a big house, and a Buick or Cadillac instead of a Chevrolet, I decided I'd become successful as a way of proving that I really mattered.

By my mid 20s, things were looking really good. I had graduated from one of the country's top schools, married a former beauty queen, was working in a promising engineering career with the Ford Motor Company, drove a bright red convertible sports car, and "owned" a great home in an upscale Detroit suburb.

I essentially had everything Madison Avenue tells us that it takes to be happy. But I wasn't. I still suffered from low self-esteem. Besides that, my marriage was failing, I disliked my job – I mean, since it had failed to provide the sense of value I craved, it was no more than a paycheck – and I had formed several bad habits, destructive to me and to those I loved, that my willpower had been unable to overcome.

Looking for answers, my wife Ginny and I decided to try church. There I was reminded of things that I had heard as a boy of 10 or 11 during the short time my mother and I regularly attended church. Among these "things" was the revelation that far from being a cosmic killjoy, God loves us and has a wonderful plan for our lives, a plan that doesn't include a bad marriage, low self-esteem, lack of purpose, and addiction to habits. So what prevents us from experiencing God's love and plan? Pure and simple, it's the fact that we've broken God's law - stealing, lying, lusting, etc.

Even as a boy God's offer of unconditional love pushed away by my sin had the ring of truth for me. So when I heard that "God so loved the world that he gave his one and only Son that whoever believes in him shall not perish but have eternal life," a decision to trust Jesus as my savior seemed like a no-brainer (see Appendix B).

Within a few months after I made that decision, my mother and I, due to an unfortunate series of circumstances, dropped out of church. For the next 15 years I lived as though I was the master of my fate and God really didn't exist. The result was the frustrating life described above.

Not long after we got back into church I made a second decision concerning God. He was already my savior, but this time I surrendered control of my life to him; I asked him to become my "CEO," i.e., to guide me by his scriptures and to empower me by his Spirit to become the man he intended me to be. It was this decision that ultimately made all the difference for me.

Over time, as I more and more allowed God to direct my thoughts and actions, my life began to change. Conscious of my friendship with God, who sacrificed his own Son for me, I experienced a renewed sense of value and worth. My marriage was transformed because God enabled me to truly love my wife and serve her. Now that I was working for God, representing him on the job, my career took on a new and satisfying purpose. God empowered me to begin dealing with my destructive habits. Best of all, based on God's promise of forgiveness and eternal life, I began living with the sure hope that when I die, I'll go to be with him forever.

Appendix B

Reflection

The underlying theme of each of these *Pointers*, whatever subject they may address, is the importance of "fearing the Lord," in Proverbs' parlance, or, in New Testament terms, of having a personal relationship to God. The scripture declares that it is through this relationship alone that we gain heaven in the future and God's aid to live an abundant life now.

The following four principles will help you discover how to know God personally and experience the abundant life he promised.

1: God loves you and created you to know him personally. He has a wonderful plan for your life. – John 3:16; John 17:3

Because he loves us, God sent his Son into the world to make it possible for us to experience eternal life, which includes not only heaven when we die, but also a fulfilling and satisfying life now.

What prevents us from knowing God personally?

2: People are sinful and separated from God, so we cannot know him personally or experience his love and plan. –Romans 3:23; John 6:23

People were created for friendship with God; but, because of stubborn self-will, we chose to go our own independent way, creating a great gulf between us and God. This self-will, characterized by an attitude of rebellion or passive indifference, is evidence of what the Bible calls sin.

Because people are irresistibly religious, we are continually trying to reach God and the fulfilling life through the "do" plan, i.e., by living a good life, having the right philosophy or being religious. But we inevitably fail.

The third principle explains the only way to bridge this gulf...

3: Jesus Christ is God's only provision for our sin. Through him alone we can know God personally and experience God's love and plan. – Romans 5:8; 1 Corinthians 15:3-6; John 14:6

Of all the faith systems only Christianity is not based on the "do" plan. It is based instead on the "done" plan–God has bridged the gulf that separates us from him by sending his Son, Jesus Christ, to die on the cross in our place to pay the penalty for our sins.

It is not enough just to know these truths...

4: We must individually receive Jesus Christ as savior; then we can know God personally and experience his love and plan. –John 1:12; Ephesians 2:8-9; John 3:1-8

John 1:12 says that God reserves the right to become his children for those who through faith receive his Son Jesus into their lives. Receiving Christ involves turning to God from self (repentance) and trusting Christ to come into our lives to forgive our sins and to make us what he wants us to be. We have to take a step of faith, as we do in every decision we make in life. After taking this step, we can know beyond any doubt, based on the authority of God's Word, that Christ lives in us and that we have eternal life.

If you want to take this step of faith yourself, you can receive Christ right now through prayer. God knows your heart and is not so concerned with your words as he is with the attitude of your heart. The following is a suggested prayer:

Lord Jesus, I want to know you personally. Thank you for dying on the cross for my sins. I open the door of my life and receive you as my savior. Thank you for forgiving me of my sins and giving me eternal life. Take control of my life. Make me the kind of person you want me to be.

Does this prayer express the desire of your heart? It if does, pray this prayer right now, and Christ will come into your life, as he promised.

If you have come to know Christ personally through this presentation of the gospel or would like further help in getting to know Christ better, two sites are recommended: www.startingwithGod.com or www.LooktoJesus.com.

CPSIA information can be obtained
at www.ICGtesting.com
Printed in the USA
FSOW02n1609120416
19122FS

9 781498 469814